Successor States and Cooperation Theory

SUCCESSOR STATES AND COOPERATION THEORY

A Model for Eastern Europe

George Macesich

PRAEGER

Westport, Connecticut
London

HC
244
M2242
1994

Library of Congress Cataloging-in-Publication Data

Macesich, George.
    Successor states and cooperation theory : a model for Eastern
Europe / George Macesich.
        p.   cm.
    Includes bibliographical references (p.   ) and index.
    ISBN 0–275–94936–2 (alk. paper)
        1. Europe, Eastern—Economic integration.   2. Post-communism—
Europe, Eastern.   3. Capitalism—Europe, Eastern.   4. Democracy—
Europe, Eastern.   I. Title.
HC244.M2242   1994
337.1'47—dc20   94–6377

British Library Cataloguing in Publication Data is available.

Library of Congress Catalog Card Number: 94–6377
ISBN: 0–275–94936–2

First published in 1994

Praeger Publishers, 88 Post Road West, Westport, CT 06881
An imprint of Greenwood Publishing Group, Inc.

Printed in the United States of America

The paper used in this book complies with the
Permanent Paper Standard issued by the National
Information Standards Organization (Z39.48–1984).

10 9 8 7 6 5 4 3 2 1

To

Bernard F. Sliger

Scholar, Colleague, and Friend

Contents

Preface

This book addresses the problems of successor states in Central and East Europe and their transformation into market democracies. It discusses the important issues involved in such transformation with the aid of economic theory and cooperation theory. It argues that the transformation of successor states into functioning market democracies can be facilitated by drawing upon and incorporating the lessons of cooperation theory as well as standard economic theory. By doing so, the successor states are more likely to achieve the fruits and benefits of market democracy so long denied their citizens. In effect, the book draws upon and extends the theory of cooperation of issues of successor states and their problems of reform and transition to market democracies. It weaves together institutional, theoretical, and empirical results of game theory and policy analysis, so that each reinforces the other. Only when many strands are woven together can we have a useful understanding of an issue as complex as the transformation of a hitherto tightly controlled society into a market democracy. This volume is directed to policy makers with key roles in the transformation processes—general economists, political scientists, and lay persons. It is particularly important that nonspecialists understand the issues, since movement toward market democracy involves building a broad base of support.

I am indebted to many colleagues with whom I have discussed one or another aspect of this study over the years. These include the more than 1,000 scholars and students who participated in the Florida State University Center for Yugoslav-American Studies, Research and

Exchanges and its joint program of Comparative Policy Studies in the
period between 1961 and 1993. Foremost among them are Marshall R.
Colberg, Walter Macesich, Jr., Milton Friedman, Anna J. Schwartz,
Branimir M. Janković, Dragomir Vojnić, Ljubisav Marković, Ljubiša
Adamović, Stojan Bulat, Dimitrije Dimitrijević, and Rikard Lang. On
this score Bernard F. Sliger deserves special mention. It is to him that
this book is dedicated.

I would also like to express appreciation for editorial and other
assistance to Dr. Carol Bullock, Esther C. S. Glenn, and Beverly
McNeil.

Successor States and Cooperation Theory

1

Is Small Beautiful?

UNITY AND PEACE THROUGH DIVISION?

Political disintegration and secession are redefining the map of Europe. A loose commonwealth of independent countries and Russia replaced the Soviet Union. The Baltic states of Lithuania, Estonia, and Latvia have declared their independence. Yugoslavia as a smaller entity continues to exist. Four of Yugoslavia's republics—Croatia, Slovenia, Macedonia, and Bosnia-Herzegovina—have declared their independence. The Czecho-Slovak federation is dissolved.

Even in the Serb-populated parts of Croatia and in South Ossetia in the former Soviet republic of Georgia, there are independence movements within independent governments. Indeed, this call for self-determination will continue to be heard from Scotland to Brittany, to Provence, to Bavaria, to Sicily, and to the Basque homeland of Euskadi.

These developments can be positive, if indeed "small is beautiful." For example, there is no relationship between growth or level of per capita income and the size of a country, whether measured by population or area. Even small countries, with populations of under a million, can perform economically, as long as they remain open to international trade. As a matter of fact, these countries tend to encourage external trade and ties because to discourage them would be far too costly.

There is also little relationship between a country's endowment of key natural resources and development. For example, consider Japan, Hong Kong, and other countries without such key resources as oil. A country can compensate for the lack of these resources through international trade.

As many observers have noted, the key resources are a good government and a pluralistic democracy in a free market society, with private property and civil rights transcending narrow nationalism, where everyone has the freedom to develop. In effect, it is the acceptance of a market democracy by government and the people, which in itself is the culmination of more than 300 years of economic and political thought.[1] Market democracy does not share the Marxist pretension that commandeering society is the one way to assure prosperity and freedom. It is equally skeptical of the nationalism that has replaced Marxism in many of these countries as the guiding spirit of government.

In fact, some writers recommend that Europe should be broken up into almost sovereign cantonal arrangements on the Swiss model. Cooperation would be based on the smallness of all states rather than on the collaboration of powerful nations.[2] Switzerland is given as an example of a small state which has thrived not only because of its material unity but because of the smallness of its cells. Not only are a number of these cells democratic, almost sovereign cantons, but they also have low cantonal populations, which makes it difficult for any one canton to dominate the others. Here we have a model of unity and peace through division. The possibility of war among these micro-states tends to be minor in comparison to the events of 1941 and certainly less threatening to the world. However, no war is minor to the people involved.

Within a historical context, the nation-state is indeed a comparative newcomer. Germany and Italy made the transition to this arrangement only in the middle of the nineteenth century, while the former Soviet Union, Yugoslavia, India, and others made the transition more recently. When measured by the rhetoric of these countries and their successor states, a sense of nationhood may not yet be sufficiently secure for their acceptance as a political reality.

If successor states are to successfully transform themselves into working market economies, they must adopt a strategy for doing so. They are well advised to draw on cooperation theory and a strategy of Tit-for-Tat for the task at hand. It is considered a "nice" strategy. It is a strategy of cooperating on the first move and then doing what the other player did on the preceding move. In effect, it is a strategy of cooperation based on reciprocity. Such a strategy, moreover, can work even in a hostile environment created by ethnic and nationalist strife. It can promote the transformation of successor states into market democracies and the peaceful coexistence of people with sharply different national identities.

MULTIPLE ARRANGEMENTS

The multiplicity of political arrangements we call a nation and the difficulty in defining it are clear enough. Shall we define the nation in terms of tribe, ethnicity, race, language, religion, or locality? Should we use some or all of these terms? The political will and economic welfare of a people ultimately determine how they want to govern themselves. Political evolution through different legal forms had as its central concern the legitimacy of government and the happiness of the governed.

In a world of more economically interdependent regions, nations, even if united, may be obsolete. The European community arrangements and the commonwealth arrangement of Russia and the former Soviet states are now phases in a more open process, which will force us to give a new meaning to the term *political convenience.*

An arrangement of micro-states within a European community would serve to restrain the perceived ambitions of a united Germany. Whether or not we shall have a German Europe of a Kaiser or a Hitler or the European Germany of a Thomas Mann remains to be seen.

The unilateral recognition of Slovenia and Croatia by Germany in spite of objections raised by the United States, France, Britain, and the United Nations bodes ill for future European affairs. To many observers, the warning signs are there for a reconstituted German sphere of influence from Talinin (Estonia) in the north to Zagreb (Croatia) in the south or, in essence, from the Baltic to the Adriatic.

Despite talk of European unity, it appears that a predominantly German sphere of influence is being reconstituted in Central and Eastern Europe that the United States, Britain, and France may find difficult to penetrate. A Europe united under German domination will not see Britain and France surrender their sovereignty to such a Europe. The model for a Europe of the future may not necessarily be the political model now envisioned but rather a reflection of the age-old search for a balance of power that prevents any one nation from dominating Europe.

However, other analysts are more optimistic, pointing out that what is striking thus far is not the *strength* of an intolerant nationalism but rather its *weakness.*[3] For now in the most important successor states of Ukraine and Russia, nationalism has taken a rather moderate form. Ukraine's stand on granting citizenship to all, regardless of ethnicity or language, is reassuring, especially to the large number of ethnic Russians who voted for its independence. Perhaps it is correct to believe that the issue is not mindless nationalism but rather the desire for political freedom and a move from the old communist center—a similar pattern detected in communist countries.

INTERPLAY BETWEEN NATIONALISM AND DEMOCRACY

Still, the interplay between nationalism and democracy is delicate. The failure of democracy in Germany in the 1920's and 1930's caused the world untold misery. Can we be sure that the newly minted "democrats" will be able to or even desire to consolidate a liberal form of nationalism with the daunting task of converting controlled economies to market-based ones? It is not clear how these newly independent states will walk that fine line between assertiveness on legitimate national identity and intolerance.

Nationalism is often a crucial means for empowering communities to take control of their own destinies in order to liberate themselves from the tyranny of undemocratic forms of government. Once national identities are securely established, perhaps nationalist passions will subside enough to permit the emergence of stable democracies based on liberal political principles. Then the problem will be of how to make the ever-present "national" identity compatible with democracy.

Not all analysts are optimistic that the two can be made compatible. The more pessimistic argue that the collapse of totalitarian regimes in Europe would only encourage an intolerant nationalism serving various proto-fascist demagogues. There is skepticism of nascent democracies headed by newly discovered "democrats" whose policy prescription for balance-of-power politics is designed to provide world security.

LESSONS LEARNED FROM WORLD WAR I

We can draw some important lessons from the economic and political dislocation that followed World War I. Germany and Central Europe vividly demonstrate what can go wrong if correct policies are not followed and of the important role the rest of the world can play.

In 1919 and in 1991, an empire was broken up: In 1919 the Austro-Hungarian empire; in 1991 the Soviet Union and Yugoslavia dissolved. New successor states came on the world stage. New republics were formed and new governments struggled to assert their authority. In the former Soviet Union, taxes were not collected, and public spending rose, while governments continued to pay large inherited bureaucracies and responded to domestic public pressures. The result was uncontrolled government deficits. With responsibility to no government, the surviving central bank of the Austro-Hungarian empire took temporary measures and printed money without restraint. From 1991 to 1992, the central banks also continued to print rubles and dinars and issued cheap credit unchecked in the former Soviet Union and in a disintegrating Yugoslavia. These policies had to be restrained if hyperinflation was to be averted.

During the 1920's, hyperinflation came very quickly. The German case was the most dramatic.[4] By late 1923, prices rose by 41,000 percent each month. In 1922, inflation in the Austrian republic rose from 5 percent to 80 percent per month. However, other examples less affected by war debt are more relevant for the 1990's.[5]

Hyperinflation in the Central European republics was eventually stopped during the 1920's, but not before it left irreparable political scars. Governments were able to stabilize their economies once control over their budgets was reasserted. Central banks were made independent of their government's treasuries.

Coordinated international intervention was critical to success. The fiscal and monetary reforms that stopped inflation in Austria in August 1922 are an example. After the Council of the League of Nations agreed to guarantee support and some financial aid, the government was able to carry out desperately needed domestic reforms. With the Austrians agreeing to eliminate their budget deficit and to create an autonomous central bank, the League of Nations then agreed to guarantee the republic's border and committed itself to debt rescheduling and additional aid. When the announcement of the agreement was made, inflation came to a screeching halt before its details became public and before implementation began.

The first lesson from the experience of the 1920's is that runaway hyperinflation is likely to be produced by continuing economic and political crisis. The second lesson is that international support of the currency is initially required to make the exchange rate credible.

An example of the problem faced by many of these countries is provided by the Russian central bank whose difficulties reflect the evolution of banking in Russia. Prior to 1991, state-owned banks essentially distributed money allocated by the government; however, by 1992 most of those banks had been turned into enterprises. Although the Russian government still holds a majority of the shares, it operates as if it were independent by raising money to make loans to state and private enterprises. Most of the banks that loan primarily to farmers and to agricultural equipment companies do not take deposits but depend instead on loans from the central bank. The money is then reloaned at interest rates higher than those charged by the central bank.

By early 1992, the money-losing agricultural sector had not repaid the commercial banks nor had they repaid the central bank. This action left the central bank with the option of either calling in its loans, refraining from issuing additional credit, or continuing to finance the agricultural sector in order to guarantee that the country could feed itself. Direct government subsidies to agriculture are impossible because of the huge budget deficit.

By pulling back on credit in Russia, it means that the central bank must print fewer rubles. Fewer rubles means the currency is more valuable and thus more easily converted into hard currencies. In turn, a strong, easily convertible ruble would attract foreign investment, encourage experts, and make imports easier to purchase. All are goals sought by the International Monetary Fund (IMF) and indeed the Russian reform government.

NOTES

1. George Macesich, *Reform and Market Democracy* (New York: Praeger, 1991).

2. John McClanghry, "A Visionary of Disunion," *New York Times*, 28 December 1991, p. 13.

3. Francis Fukuyama, "Rest Easy, It's Not 1914 Anymore," *New York Times*, 9 February 1992, p. 17.

4. Phillip Cagan, "The Monetary Dynamics of Hyperinflation," in *Studies in the Quantity Theory of Money*, ed. Milton Friedman (Chicago: University of Chicago Press, 1956), 25-117.

5. George Macesich, *World Banking and Finance: Cooperation Versus Conflict* (New York: Praeger, 1984).

2

Coincidence of Troubles and Lack of Cooperation: Lessons from the Inter-War Period

The need for cooperation, along with a "nice strategy," in dealing with issues and problems that transcend country borders is perhaps best illustrated in the Great Depression. This chapter focuses on the monetary features of this tragic chain of events as they were manifested in Europe, and especially Great Britain, Canada, Yugoslavia, and the United States. The collapse of the international monetary and financial structures forever modified the economic, political, and social systems of most countries. The demise of communism and the transition to market democracy in the former socialist countries is as important to the world today as were events of the 1930's. Once again, the need for cooperation and a "nice strategy" is underscored.

COINCIDENCE OF TROUBLES: "CAUSES" OF THE GREAT DEPRESSION

Although the National Bureau of Economic Research dates the Great Depression from June 1929 to March 1933, the economic, social, and political reverberations of that debacle completely dominated the remaining years of the 1930's and exerted a strong influence on the thinking of at least two generations.[1] The economic consequences of the depression were truly awesome. In the United States, unemployment soared to the rate of nearly 25 percent of the labor force in 1933. Gross national product fell from $104.4 billion in 1929 to a depression low of $74.2 billion in 1933. Not until 1937 was the 1929 level to be regained only to fall once more in the recession of 1938.

The falloff in aggregate demand led not only to declines in production, but also to widespread price deflation. Wholesale prices dropped to nearly one half of what they had been in 1929. Retail prices fell less sharply, but nevertheless by about one-fourth between 1929 and 1933. It was not until World War II that prices regained their 1929 level. For the typical American, disposable personal income fell from $683 in 1929 to $362 in 1933.

In Canada, money, prices, and income contracted sharply during the 1930–1933 period.[2] The exchange rate, however, remained buoyant. A combination of factors explain the failure of the Canadian dollar to depreciate against the American dollar and the British pound following the country's *de facto* departure from the gold standard in the early part of 1929, the year the Department of Finance informally terminated the unrestricted convertibility of Dominion notes—a fact recognized formally in 1931. In the first place, Canada gave the appearance of continuing to follow the roles for preservation of fixed exchange rates and the maintenance of external balance even though it was no longer on the gold standard. One effect of such efforts was to maintain the confidence of foreigners in the Canadian economy, thereby avoiding a speculative outflow of capital. In the second place, a net inflow of capital occurred at this time. In the third place, the protective tariff was raised so that the demand for foreign exchange was lessened. These factors eased but did not eliminate Canadian difficulties.

In Yugoslavia the gross national product declined from 1930 through 1933 as did national income and per capita income. The total stock of money declined by almost 20 percent in the same period. The value of Yugoslavia's foreign trade was almost halved in the 1930–1934 period, and internal prices declined by over 20 percent.

Much has been said about this important episode in world history which we now call the Great Depression, and more will be. Some people argue that the depression was inevitable. The basis for their view is not always clear, except apparently, bad times must follow good times. Others hold that after a certain time prosperity destroys itself and depression corrects itself. These views are not supported by the available evidence of the 1920's and 1930's. Nothing in the cyclical nature of the American economy, nor indeed in the world economy, required the collapse and stagnation of the 1930's. Consumers and producers apparently stood ready to support continued economic expansion during this critical post–World War I period.

Other likely candidates for proximate causes of the 1929 debacle can be readily enumerated.[3] For example, insufficient advance in investment contributed to high interest rates and could have generated a decline in total demand for goods and services, and/or weak sectors such as agriculture could have served to transmit trouble to the economy as a whole. An unequal distribution of income in which presumably the rich were getting richer and the poor poorer placed the economy in a precarious position in that it required a high level of investment in luxuries, newer plants, and equipment—all highly volatile and subject to erratic influences.

A poor corporate structure, in the view of some observers, made the American economy sensitive to any interruption in the flow of dividends from operating companies. According to this argument, the 1920's produced a vast array of holding companies and investment trusts which in effect pyramided the American corporate structure. Dividends from operating companies paid the interest on the bonds of the upstream holding companies. Any interruption in the flow of dividends from operating companies produced defaults on bonds, bankruptcy, and the collapse of the structure. As a result, a strong incentive existed to curtail investment in operating plants in order to continue dividends, thereby adding to the deflationary pressures. These pressures, in turn, reduced earnings and brought down the corporate structure. One consequence was even more retrenchment. Income was earmarked by debt repayment, making borrowing for new investments highly unlikely. This system was almost perfectly designed to accentuate and perpetuate a downward spiral.

The wobbly structure of the American banking system is another good candidate. The large number of independent banks without adequate deposit insurance encouraged a domino effect when one bank failed. Depositors demanded their money from banks whose assets were frozen. The situation was not helped when the Federal Reserve System failed in its function as "lender of last resort."

The foreign trade sector in the post–World War I years provides another likely source of trouble. It was in this period that the United States became a creditor on international account. A monetary and fiscal policy (including high tariffs) coupled with traditional and historical habits accounted for a persistently favorable trade balance in American dealings with other countries. Previously, payments on interest and principal had in effect been deducted from the trade balance. In the post–World War I years they were added to the favorable American balance. Thus countries that were buying more than they were selling and had debt payments to make covered the difference in gold payments and/or new loans. Such an arrangement provided only a short-term solution. In the long run countries could not cover their adverse trade balances with the United States in gold or new loans. They either had to increase their exports to the United States (made difficult by sharply increased American tariffs) or reduce their imports and/or default on their loans. By not playing according to the "rules of the gold standard game," the Americans forced more of the burden of international adjustment on foreigners.

We can also add to the probable list of causes the catastrophic advice offered by so-called sound and responsible experts both within and outside government who urged a balanced budget even if such a budget required reduced governmental outlays and increased taxes at the very time when an opposite policy was required.[4] This is tantamount to a rejection of both fiscal and monetary policy. Those urging an affirmative government economic policy had neither the unanimity nor the authority to force the American government to check deflation and depression.

From the results obtained for the United States, Canada, Yugoslavia, and some other countries, it appears that the income velocity of money is empirically stabler than the investment multiplier in all periods for which the results are available except during the early years of the Great Depression after 1929.[5] It is of considerable interest to note that the Keynesian Revolution with its de-emphasis on the importance of the stock of money occurred during the 1930's and almost precisely at the time when the simple version of the income expenditure theory achieved its best historical performance.

It is true, of course, that statistical correlations by themselves tell us nothing about the direction of cause and effect. Close correlation between money and income does not necessarily mean that the direction of causality is from money to income. Indeed, such correlation may also mean that causality is from income to money, or perhaps even the result of a common third factor. These and still other causes are clearly possibilities. Additional studies other than those purely statistical in character are needed to judge the direction of causality. Some of these studies have already been conducted. They suggest that on occasion changes in the supply of money can be separated from contemporary changes in income.[6] For example, changes in the money supply brought about by currency reforms, gold discoveries, and political uncertainty are hardly associated with income changes.

It is the incredible coincidence of troubles in the post–World War I period that presents us with the "third factor" and the fundamental disturbance-creating changes in the money supply which were indeed separate from contemporary changes in income. Reluctance on the part of Britain to come to terms with its diminished status on the world scene and its persistence in pursuing a forlorn policy of first a return to gold at the pre-war par and then with the maintenance of the gold standard at a fixed rate set in motion the "third factor," which served to separate money and income. Confident that they knew best how to play the gold standard game, the British were reluctant to capitulate to American dominance in international finance even if the latter were seriously willing to entertain such dominance.[7] British pride, prestige, and indeed the Empire were at stake. Neither the Bank of England nor British governments of any party would have been willing to accept responsibility for facilitating the smooth transfer of such power to the inexperienced and indifferent Americans.

Nevertheless, the American role in the gold standard game after 1918 was critical.[8] The Americans required careful cultivation if the game was to be played with any hope of success. The distribution of gold reserves had changed dramatically. These reserves increased in the United States from 692 million dollars in 1913 to more than 2.5 billion dollars in 1921. By comparison, Great Britain's reserves increased by 583 million dollars in the same period. The situation for the major European industrial countries was even less favorable; for example, France gained about 10 million dollars in gold reserves during this period and Germany lost about 18 million dollars.

The dollar's supremacy on every European exchange with free American coinage and no restrictions on either import or export of gold convinced many people that only the dollar was a real gold currency. Indeed, since the American resumption of specie payments in 1879, gold's price appeared constant at around $20.67 per fine ounce. It is not surprising, therefore, that until 1925 the dollar served as an international standard against which all other currencies fluctuated.

To the displeased London bankers anxious to regain their pre-1914 position in world finance, the years of dollar supremacy were at the very best a trial. It was simply assumed that Great Britain would return to the gold standard at the pre-war parity of the pound. This was an article of faith. The Cunliffe Committee in 1918 estimated that the transition to normal monetary conditions would take some ten years. For such a restoration a difficult post-war deflation in Britain was to be accepted. It was also expected that the process of adjustemnt would be aided by further inflation in the United States. This was not to be. The British were appalled to find that the Federal Reserve Board was simply not following accepted "rules of the game" of the gold standard.[9] The Americans did not expand to accommodate the British and the rest of the world.[10] They simply calculated the requirements for internal domestic balance inflated accordingly and sterilized excess gold reserves.

The Cunliffe Committee not only miscalculated American reaction but also misjudged internal British political events as to the acceptance of internal deflation for the sake of specie resumption at pre-war par.[11] The labor unrest that followed contributed in time to the disintegration of the British Empire.

It will be recalled that John Maynard Keynes since about 1924 had advocated public works in a supporting role to monetary policy as an anti-deflationary device. From the behavior of the Bank of England and its determination to accept and enforce whatever price fluctuations were consistent, first with the return to gold at the pre-war par and then with the maintenance of the gold standard at a fixed rate, Keynes became convinced that Great Britain would have to rely on means other than monetary policy to stabilize internal prices and output. Monetary disturbances led to variations in output through price changes and their influence on expectations of future prices. Keynes argued that the relation between current and future prices influences investment decisions most. In a world of rapidly fluctuating prices, uncertainty on the part of businessmen would be so great that the government would have to undertake the investment necessary for growth and economic stability. Keynes thus moved from reliance on monetary to fiscal policy on grounds that it was politically unrealistic to expect stable growth in the money supply.

SEARCH FOR NORMALCY: MUDDLING THROUGH

Prior to World War I, Western Europe and particularly Great Britain had served as the center for a worldwide trading system financed largely through the London money market.[12] The 1920's witnessed a change, with Europe no longer functioning as the world's banker. Imports increased relative to exports, producing balance-of-payments difficulties for most European countries. Increasing amounts of income for investments overseas went to pay for imports and left little income out of which to advance capital loans to borrowing countries. At this point the United States stepped in and replaced Europe as the world's banker. Large American loans were readily extended to Germany during the 1920's. Other countries also borrowed in the millions of dollars for reconstruction and development.

Unfortunately for world trade and the international gold standard, the United States did not qualify as a sophisticated world banker. American banks readily lent large sums. The economic policy of the United States, however, placed major obstacles in the way of repayment of loans. In view of its status as a major creditor nation, the United States should logically have increased its imports in order to enable other countries to earn dollars so as to service their debt to the United States. One important way, of course, is to lower American import tariffs. The United States did just the opposite; it increased tariffs in 1922 (Fordney-McCumber Tariff) and again in 1930 (Smoot-Hawley Tariff), thereby boosting protectionism to its highest levels in American history.[13] Other countries paid the interest on their debts to the United States temporarily out of further loans rather than from increased productivity associated with foreign loans and shifts in world production.

The entire foreign trade and debt issue was further complicated by American insistence upon repayment of war debts. High tariffs, however, meant that the United States did not welcome payment of war debts in goods. Moreover, there was not enough gold outside the United States for payment of debts. Allied insistence that Germany pay reparations rested in part in the Allies' desire to use the proceeds to pay war debts to the United States.

Improved arrangements known as the Dawes Plan (1924) and the Young Plan (1929) facilitated debt financing. The United States made concessions to the Allies by lowering the rate of interest at which the war debts accumulated. Between 1924 and 1929 all seemed to go quite well. Germany was able to make reparations payments and the Allies to make war debt payments according to schedule.

However, the entire debt arrangement was wobbly and indeed illusory. The fact is that American private investors were making large dollar loans to Germany. The Germans, in turn, used the dollars to pay reparations, and the Allies used the dollars to pay war debts. In short, the United States was paying itself. Given the dollar magnitude of the debt involved, this was not correct; but it was used by those in favor of cancellation of debts to support their case.

This international financial circus was brought to a sudden end by the Great Depression of 1929 when American loans to Germany ceased. German industry, however, had been reconstructed and strengthened, but democratic government in Germany had been undermined partly over the reparations issue. International relations among wartime Allies as well as between Germany and allies had become embittered. In effect, attempts to collect war debts and to make reparations payments proved to be one colossal failure. It was an experiment which was not to be repeated in the post–World War II period.

If the international gold standard was to operate properly, the "flow of gold" or equivalent into the United States should have raised domestic American prices. Higher American prices would have made American goods and services more expensive relative to foreign goods and services, thereby increasing imports relative to exports in the United States. At the same time, a rise in American domestic prices would have permitted adjustment in the international value of the British pound without the agonizing deflation which kept Great Britain in a straitjacket between 1924 and 1931. The fact is, however, on price policy as on tariffs policy the United States undermined the "rules" on the international gold standard. Stable domestic prices rather than stable international exchange rates was the goal pursued by the Federal Reserve System, thereby jeopardizing the long-run future of the gold standard. American failure to raise prices prevented the necessary shifts in world production.

The early victims of the wobbly world financial and economic structure were the countries producing foodstuffs and raw materials. In order to meet their balance of payments deficits, they threw wave after wave of products on world markets for whatever they could get. They cut down on imports wherever possible and pushed their exports in crumbling world markets. As the prices for their products declined, the real burden of their debts increased significantly.

A case in point is the depressed agricultural countries of America and Europe (including Canada and Yugoslavia). Confronted with collapsing export prices, they borrowed on a short-term basis from Vienna and Berlin, which in turn had borrowed from London to pay for debt services and imports. Had the depression quickly abated, such short-term borrowing would have been justified. The worldwide situation, unfortunately, deteriorated rapidly.

World money markets failed in May 1931, when the largest bank in Austria, the Credit-Anstalt, failed, a victim of the default on loans made to the depressed economies of Europe. From Vienna to Berlin, to London and New York the catastrophe spread. German banks were sensitive to the Austrian money market owing to the fact that they had re-lent large sums borrowed on a short-term basis from London. The German situation, moreover, was already precarious because of the cutoff of American loans in 1929. During the early months of 1931, the Reichs Bank lost nine-tenths of its gold reserve. In July 1931, all foreign payments by Germans were suspended, with 10 billion Reichmarks of short-term credit owed to foreign creditors, mostly London.

Suspension of payments by Germany meant that British credits were frozen and could not be collected. Many foreigners, including the central banks of countries operating on a gold exchange standard, held large short-term deposits in London. These depositors became alarmed and withdrew heavily from England. The bank of England lost more than 200 million £ in gold within two months after the German "freeze" in July. Indeed, between Wednesday and Saturday in the third week of September, 43 million £ of gold were lost. On September 20, 1931, the Bank of England suspended gold payments and Great Britain went off the gold standard.

Many countries quickly followed Great Britain off the gold standard. Only France and the United States among the large nations and Switzerland, Belgium, and the Netherlands among the smaller nations remained on gold for the time being.

France and the United States held most of the world gold surplus reserves. Indeed, French gold reserves had been rising rapidly, from 5.9 billion (pre-devaluation) francs in June 1928 to 36.6 billion in June 1929, 43.9 billion in June 1920, 56.3 billion in June 1931, and 81.2 billion in June 1932. They reached a high of 32 billion francs in December 1932. The French were not particularly disturbed that their actions in acquiring these gold reserves placed an additional deflationary burden on the rest of the world. In fact, French commentators and the public congratulated themselves for remaining true to the gold standard. Of course, one consequence was that as the prices of products of these countries began to fall relative to French and American products, their export industries suffered, ushering in attempts to rescue their industries by creating ever-higher tariffs.

But even France and the United States could not escape for long. By the end of June 1932, the United States lost nearly $2 billion in gold. Foreign withdrawals plus increasing domestic demand for gold caused by shrinking credit led to a gold crisis. More than 5,000 banks failed in the United States between 1930 and 1932. Following a temporary closing of all banks in March 1933, the United States suspended gold payments and for all practical purposes departed from the gold standard in 1934.

Belgium went off the gold standard in 1935, followed by France, Switzerland, and the Netherlands in 1936. The international financial and monetary structure erected over the course of a century prior to 1914 and so painfully "restored" following World War I collapsed within a decade or so after its restoration. With it perished worldwide economic solidarity and confidence in international solutions to economic problems. Henceforth problems would be solved on a national level. Beggar-thy-neighbor policies in the form of protective tariffs, import quotas, and exchange controls became the rule. Nationalistic solutions simply aggravated the depression, and month by month between January 1929 and June 1933 the volume of world trade declined.

Charles Kindleberger has put it well that "for the world economy to be stabilized there has to be a stabilizer, one stabilizer" (quoted in *Wall Street Journal*, October 23, 1979, p. 1). Britain between the wars was unable to do it and the United States apparently could not and/or would not.

British impotence on this score is best described by Sir Maurice Hankey writing in his diary on September 5, 1931:

> We are living just now through the most serious crisis since
> the war and the future outlook is black. After the war we

failed to adopt the measures of economy necessary to a nation
that had dissipated a large part of its wealth in smoke and
explosions. The beginning of it all was Ll. G.'s election speech
in 1919 about "a home for heroes to live in"—as I have more
than once noted in this journal.   Thereafter it has been a
"rake's progress" for which each successive Government has its
share of responsibility.[14]

Commenting on Hankey's views, Roswell writes that:

> Hankey went on to quote, approvingly, André Siegfried's
> recently published book *La Crise Britannique au 20ᵐᵉ Siècle*,
> and to recount how the crisis could be said to have begun with
> the proposal for an Austro-German Customs Union.   The
> French saw in this move the first step towards the "Anschluss"
> between Germany and Austria which was forbidden by the
> Peace Treaties. They therefore refused to offer any credits to
> Austria until the Customs Union proposal was dropped.
> Hankey wrote that "outwardly" the British government
> presented "rather a cautious attitude," but "the real opinion of
> the government was that finance should not be mixed up with
> politics." He gave no indication, however, of how the two
> could be kept separate. When the Bank of England "gave an
> accommodation to Austria without political conditions" he
> remarked to Snowden's Private Secretary that the Bank would
> lose its money; for his trip to Vienna in the previous year had
> left him with "a very bad impression of the financial and
> economic stability of the country." According to Hankey the
> French were "a good deal annoyed" by the British attitude
> towards the Austro-German Customs Union.
>   The German economic collapse and the Hoover moratori-
> um of 20th June, remitting Allied debts for a year, followed.
> Though the London Conference "extended the moratorium to
> Germany and reparations" it brought only "a temporary
> alleviation"; and the German failure to repay short-term
> credits granted by Britain and their inability to pay "Bills for
> imports as they matured in London," together with financial
> troubles in many other countries, reacted on the British
> financial position in the same way.[15]

There was and is more—much more—for the demise of British
power, especially for British Imperial power. A. P. Thornton in a
succinct study of British power attributes its decline to the fact that
nationalism, democracy, and war mounted a separate and then a

combined assault against the imperialist position, and that the supporters of Empire, lacking a sense of unity, were unable to counteract the erosion of their power.[16]

It is strange and surprising to some that the final blow to the idea of Empire came in the autumn of 1956 with the Suez Canal crisis. The delusion, for most years since 1918, circulated that somehow the United States could be coaxed into salvaging if not the French Empire then certainly the British Empire. The belief in the unique inheritance, centuries of experience with Europe, and its colonies overseas had given the British supporters of Empire the wisdom the Americans would surely come to respect. Under British tutelage and guidance, the Americans would provide the means for defending Europe and its empires. Indeed, Sir Winston Churchill talked persuasively that it was the responsibility of the United States to provide a "Pax Americana" for the twentieth century.[17] The United States was to be the monetary and economic "stabilizer," political arbiter, policeman, and whatnot for the twentieth century.

It became obvious that Americans did not envision such a role for themselves. Thus the Suez crisis demonstrates that the United States had no intention whatsoever of supporting British, French, and Israeli attempts to retake the Suez Canal and hang on to remnants of an empire. No one considered the risks such an American refusal carried for the Atlantic Alliance. The Americans understandably felt themselves badly used by their nominal allies. There simply never has been much of a following in the United States for a "Pax Americana." Such a concept did not sit well with the doctrinal heirs of Woodrow Wilson, the enemy of empires who preached "self-determination for all nations and peoples."[18] To argue that Americans failed to accept their international responsibilities is simply to misunderstand the definition of these responsibilities as viewed from the United States. A transcontinental power whose foreign trade accounts for significantly less than 10 percent of its gross national product is understandably less likely to view international responsibilities in the same way as a small island nation with a sizable foreign trade sector and an overseas empire. Simply put, when the monetary system was reconstructed following World War I, the builders would have been well advised to look elsewhere for a stabilizer than to the United States.

THE AMERICAN ROLE AS STABILIZER AND THE FEDERAL RESERVE SYSTEM

As to why Americans could not or would not act as stabilizer, we turn to the Federal Reserve's mistakes in the 1920's and 1930's, which have been discussed at some length by Milton Friedman and Anna Schwartz in *A Monetary History of the United States, 1867–1960* (see also footnote 1). The Federal Reserve's errors began when it failed to tighten money in 1919. They were compounded when tight money was applied too late, too much, and for too long in 1920. To be sure, the American monetary authorities had an explanation of each. In 1919, monetary policy was still subordinate to Treasury needs. In 1920 when the gold reserve was under pressure, the rules of orthodox central banking and the gold standard called for tight money.

During the middle twenties, the American money supply grew at a more or less regular rate, and the economy performed well. Toward the end of the twenties, however, monetary errors came with increasing frequency. It was at this point that Federal Reserve authorities made their biggest mistake by following a policy which was too easy to break the speculative boom and too tight to promote growth. This mistake was compounded by an exaggerated view of the importance of the stock market. Indeed, much more can be said about how the internecine squabble between the Federal Reserve Board and its New York bank inhibited effective measures to discourage speculation.

Had the Federal Reserve authorities exercised their ample powers, they could have cut short the tragic process of monetary deflation and banking collapse. They could have prevented the stock of money from contracting, thereby avoiding the successive liquidity crises.

As the depression wore on, more serious mistakes were made. Open market purchases were entirely inadequate to turn the tide of deflation. Even worse, the monetary authorities, in order to protect the gold stock, made the unbelievable mistake of tightening money at the depth of the trough in October 1931 by raising the rediscount rate and by open-market sales.

Given the premises and philosophy that underlay American monetary policy, the Federal Reserve System had sooner or later to run into disaster. Except by Governor B. Strong of the Federal Reserve Bank of New York from 1923–1927, little attention was paid to the money stock by those who were formulating and executing monetary policy. The overwhelming majority of the most respected and influential economists of the day believed wholeheartedly in the philosophy and policy that the Federal Reserve System followed in committing its worst mistakes. Orthodox monetary theorists were mesmerized by the gold standard, haunted by an almost pathological fear of inflation, shocked by amateur stock market speculation, and led astray by the "real bills" doctrine. When the bull market entered its most intense phase in 1927, orthodox theorists urged the Federal Reserve System to tighten money in order to eliminate speculative activity.

It is possible that the Federal Reserve's mistakes are indeed as some authors argue. In the process of protecting the economy from exaggerated dangers, policy makers may have blundered into economic disaster. I would argue that the United States was simply an unwilling stabilizer at best. President Roosevelt, for example, was not particularly keen on supporting any of the proposals of the World Economic Conference for a worldwide recovery plan. Politically, economically, and perhaps psychologically, Americans were not prepared to take on the burden of stabilizer for the rest of the world.

Climate of opinion has changed. The pursuit of fixed exchange rates and the gold standard so instrumental in past disasters has given way to a more sophisticated version of international monetary theory. Theorists concentrating on international trade are more likely to consider the stock of money as a more significant factor than hitherto. To them, the forces determining the long-run rate of growth of real income are largely independent of the long-run rate of growth in the stock of money so long as both proceed fairly smoothly. But market instability of money is accompanied by instability of economic growth. Friedman and Schwartz put it well when they say that money is "rather clearly the senior partner in longer-run movements and in major cyclical movements, and an equal partner in shorter-run and milder movements."

EFFECTS ON CANADA

By 1931 the external situation as reflected in a deficit in the Canadian balance of payments took a turn for the worse. In order to keep the exchange rate fixed, a further contraction of money, prices, and income was necessary. Although the chartered banks lost gold and external assets in attempting to support the dollar, these efforts proved inadequate. Rather than continue the internal contraction required to preserve external balance, Canada departed formally from the gold standard in October 1931, and the exchange rate depreciated significantly in terms of the United States dollar. That the exchange rate depreciation alone failed to eliminate Canadian difficulties is indicated by the decline in economic activity which continued until March 1933 when a trough was reached. During this subperiod the stock of money declined by about 8 percent and prices by approximately 10 percent.

The one particularly bright spot in Canadian experience during the period was that, contrary to the experience of the United Stats, the Canadian banking system did not collapse under the economic adjustments of the period. The chartered banks continued to contract their operations despite government attempts in November 1932 to have them do otherwise by forcing the banks to borrow, under the provisions of the Finance Act, $35 million in Dominion notes at a cost of 3 percent. The measure did not achieve the desired results because the banks proceeded to reduce their indebtedness to the government. Its effects on the stock of money appear to be negligible.

However, within a month of the attempts by the government to force chartered banks to expand, the premium on U.S. funds increased from 11 percent to 19 percent, reflecting a further depreciation of the Canadian dollar. The depreciation may be attributed in part to the uncertainty generated by the government's expansionary policy that replaced the policy of contraction. By such a reversal of policy, the government in effect promoted expectations of price increases, and thus further exchange losses, thereby confirming public suspicion of its inability to maintain fixed exchange rates and to observe rules of the game for their preservation.

The year 1934 brought an improvement in Canadian economic affairs. As a result of the depreciation, exports, which had started to recover in 1933, advanced markedly in 1934. Following the World Economic Conference, the government in 1934 attempted once more to increase the stock of money by expanding bank cash by some $53 million through the issue of Dominion notes, but this time without gold backing. The government's justification for this measure was that the conference had changed the rules of the gold standard game. Canada, on this view, was safe in expanding without worrying about exchange rate depreciation as had occurred in 1932. In effect, Canada was now free to pursue an independent monetary policy. Internal monetary changes affected the price level and through it the exchange rate. The subsequent expansion was interrupted again in 1938 when Canada experienced a decline in its exports. The difficulties originated in the short but severe recession that developed in the United States in 1937; expansion in the American economy did not resume until the latter part of 1938, but Canada was fortunate in having other foreign markets for support.

The declaration of war in September 1939 found the Canadian economy with a great deal of unused capacity. Employment was still below its 1929 peak and over 11 percent of the labor force was unemployed. As a result of the increased tempo of government expenditures, the gross national product with the first full year of the war rose to $6.7 billion or by nearly 20 percent in terms of current prices. At the very outset the government adopted an expansionist monetary policy, and the stock of money increased. The government's justification was that in view of the existing conditions of unused capacity in the country such a policy could be continued without fear of inflation.

Power to control foreign exchange and thereby foreign trade for war purposes was vested in the government's Foreign Exchange Control Board in September 1939. It marked the first time that government restriction had been placed on foreign transactions by private Canadian citizens. The stated objectives were to maintain exchange stability, conserve American dollars for the war effort, and prevent capital outflows. When the United Kingdom imposed exchange control in September 1939 in order to protect its dollar reserves and exchange rate, the multilateral exchange system which had existed in the pre-war period broke down. Canada could no longer, as it had done in the 1930's, convert sterling earned from a recurring net credit with the United Kingdom into dollars in order to meet the recurring deficit with the United States.

These measures, together with increased exports to the United States and attempts to increase American investment in Canada, did not prevent a serious deterioration in the country's dollar reserves in 1941. Following the Hyde Park Agreement in April 1941 and the integration of the Canadian and American economies for war production, a rapid expansion of Canadian reserves of dollars and gold occurred. By the end of 1945, Canadian holdings of American dollars and gold rose to $1.5 billion.

EFFECTS ON YUGOSLAVIA

The largely agricultural Balkan and Danubian countries of Europe, including Yugoslavia, had fallen into desperate financial and economic straits as a result of the worldwide depression and financial crisis of the early 1930's. They needed manufactured goods, and Germany needed food and raw materials. Moreover, the Balkan and Danubian countries constituted a relatively secure source of supply of food and raw materials in wartime. For the primary products, Germany paid high prices in terms of the local currencies. Payment was made, however, in "blocked marks," that is, marks which could be spent only in Germany. The Nazi war economy absorbed large quantities of imports and built up large debts to the Balkan and Danubian countries. Some crops were grown in special order under long-term contracts at guaranteed prices, thus reducing the agrarian countries to economic colonies of the imperialist Nazi system.

To their chagrin, the Balkan and Danubian countries discovered that Germany had little to export of the things they wanted. Having been ensnared in the Nazi trap, they dared not protest too vigorously lest the Nazis repudiate their debts and discontinue buying the crops for which there was no alternative market. It is ironic that these poor agrarian countries which were chronic debtors and in need of capital would have supplied large credits to Germany, thus occupying a position during the 1930's similar to that of the United States during the 1920's. Militarily and politically the agrarian countries were intimidated by the burgeoning Nazi war machine, which soon became the most powerful in the world. Such shabby treatment would have backfired in the long run and led to the disruption of bilateral arrangements or to the absorption of the agrarian states into the Nazi political orbit. This was not to be. By the time the Balkan and Danubian countries realized how short their end of the deal with Germany would be, the Second World War broke out.

As a small developing country, Yugoslavia's attempts to cope with the difficulties stemming from the Great Depression were limited. The government introduced a number of measures designed to reduce agricultural difficulties, including a moratorium on peasant debts in 1932 and cancellation in 1936. This did little to resolve the country's fundamental difficulties, which had their origins abroad.

German reparation payments, for example, played an important role in the Yugoslav economy between 1919 and 1931.[19] In this period reparations amounted to more than a half-billion gold marks or about 15 percent of Yugoslavia's tax receipts. The Germans delivered to Yugoslavia large quantities of railway equipment and machinery, including industrial installations. The cessation of these reparations had singularly serious repercussions in the country's economy.

Under the circumstances of the world situation, Yugoslavia could do little to help itself. In spite of the expansion of the economy which had occurred during the 1920's, the country entered the Great Depression as primarily an agricultural and raw material producer highly sensitive to external forces and pressures. As in the United States in the 1830's, in Yugoslavia in the 1930's external events dominated. The sharp decline in the United States in 1839 to 1843, for example, was produced by a cessation of capital imports and intensified by a decline in external prices created by a worldwide depression. In Yugoslavia in the 1930's a cessation of war reparations from Germany, combined with an external decline, brought about a sharp internal decline in Yugoslavia's economy.

CONCLUSION

What are the implications for economic theory and policy? It would seem that these implications are obvious. The inter-war period produced a coincidence of troubles which generated worldwide uncertainty, hostility, and suspicion, casting doubt on the ability of the two principal economic powers to preserve and maintain the international monetary standard and its associated monetary and financial framework. Great Britain was unable and the United States apparently was unwilling to act as the international stabilizer and preserver of pre-1914 monetary arrangements with fixed exchange rates and a gold standard. The net effect was to create a "third factor" which created the fundamental disturbance and led to changes in the money supply which were separate from contemporary changes in income.

From the viewpoint of economic policy, control over the stock of money appears to be critical. Walter Bagehot put it well, saying money will not control itself. So, too, did Milton Friedman, Anna Schwartz, and others in arguing that instability of money is accompanied by instability of economic growth. The fiction of "automaticity" of the pre-1914 gold standard was resorted to by central bankers to keep at bay politicians seeking to interfere with the formulation and execution of monetary policy by central bankers. The wisdom of such subterfuge leaves much to be desired. After all, the power to print money is the power to tax. In representative democracies such power is typically vested in the people and/or their representatives. It is certainly not a special preserve for central bankers. Better that monetary policy be formulated and executed in the sunshine so that money behaves in a predictable fashion.

The desire on the part of central bankers to mystify money is understandable, as is their desire to differentiate their product. Such desires, however, do not necessarily serve to create and perpetuate a stable monetary and financial framework, which the world so desperately needed, especially in the inter-war period and indeed in the period since World War II as well. Failure on the part of British central bankers to let their public in on the deflationary policy scheme for the post-war period resulted in badly misjudging the internal British political situation and public acceptance of such a policy. This mistake was subsequently compounded by misjudging American acceptance and willingness to play according to the "rules of the gold standard game."

For all practical purposes, the Bank of England had been trying to invent magical monetary schemes that might somehow hold together the decaying British empire, even though its peoples were no longer willing to provide the resources for doing so. Turning to the United States to underwrite the British Empire was simply to misunderstand how well armed Americans were with Wilsonian ideals of self-determination for all nations and peoples. Such ideals are ill suited for the perpetuation of imperial power. The American definition of international responsibility was simply at variance with that held by leading European colonial powers.

Keynes correctly judged these schemes as politically unacceptable and impracticable at the very least. As early as the mid-1920's he moved from reliance on monetary policy to fiscal policy on the grounds that it was politically unrealistic to expect stable growth in the money supply. This is not too distant from Milton Friedman and the monetarists, except that they express little confidence in the role that political authorities play in providing monetary stability and opt from both monetary and fiscal authorities to a fixed rule.

Always pragmatic, Keynes adapted his economic ideas to fit the time. Indeed, F. A. Hayek relates the following incident which summarizes Keynes' adaptability very well:

> Later a turn in the conversation made me [Hayek] ask him [Keynes] whether he was not concerned about what some of his disciples were making of his theories. After a not very complimentary remark about the persons concerned he proceeded to reassure me: those ideas had been badly needed at the time he had launched them. But I need not be alarmed: if they should ever become dangerous I could quickly rely upon him that he would again quickly swing around public opinion—indicating by a quick movement of his hand how rapidly that would be done. But three months later he was dead.[20]

Keynes was obsessed by the Versailles Treaty, which he considered a damnable and disastrous document incompatible with preserving civilization. He apparently was convinced that European civilization required support from every sector to escape decline. Germany must be brought into an alliance and defense against what he viewed as dark forces threatening European civilization.[21]

The French and other Europeans came off no better. His views of reparations and the transfer problems were in part colored by the view that the transfer of resources might have proven large enough to affect the competition between France and Germany for industrial leadership of the continent. He did not think it in British interests for such a transfer of resources to take place.

All of this was reinforced by Keynes' pronounced streak of anti-Americanism. His persistence regarding war debt cancellation is in part the counterpart to his position on reparations. He viewed war debts as a major issue in the struggle between the United States and Great Britain for financial hegemony. Indeed, it was Keynes who promoted the cancellationist position with the specious argument that money was making a circular flow whereby Americans made loans to

Germany, Germany paid reparations, and the Allies returned the money on war debt account. By 1932 he was arguing that Britain paid its own war expenses and had only borrowed money at "profiteering prices" to reloan elsewhere. According to Keynes, the war debts were "pure usury." Moreover, cancellation would signify "historic justice."

Stephen Schuker correctly points out that with Keynes' statements as background it is easier to understand why the American Congress passed the Johnson Default Act. Indeed, "not only did Keynes do much to shift Germany's just reparations burden to the Allies and to prepare the way for the resurgence of the Reich, but, on the evidence here, he did not act wholly in good faith."[22]

The times did indeed call for new ideas, including a new way of organizing the world's monetary and financial affairs. Even before 1914 some had foreseen that gold alone could not forever continue to provide the expanding supply of international liquidity needed to finance growing world trade. How slowly the world accepts new ideas is suggested by the fact that in much of the post–World War II period one of the more controversial problems has been the proposal for the creation of new international money to be used as national reserve assets.

While perhaps not striking a mother lode as some would argue, Keynes did indeed hit pay dirt in his *A Treatise on Money* and *General Theory of Employment, Interest and Money*. Such evidence as we have suggests that the simple version of Keynes' income expenditure theory achieved its best performance during the height of the Great Depression, though even the traditional monetary view holds its own as an explanation of events during those tragic years.

Was the Keynesian Revolution really necessary? Harry Johnson judges that it was not. What was necessary was for economists to apply the economics they already had. He faults the American Federal Reserve's failure to prevent a collapse of the American money supply, converting an otherwise normal trade cycle which began in 1929 into an unprecedentedly deep and prolonged depression. Keynes' *General Theory*, according to Johnson, simply detracted attention from all this background. There was no inherent deficiency of capitalism requiring a new theory and new policy prescriptions.[23]

Attempts by France to politically stabilize the successor states of the Austro-Hungarian Empire in the Balkan and Danubian region into the so-called Little Entente (Yugoslavia, Czechoslovakia, and Romania) as a prelude to achieving economic stability met with less than enthusiastic response from its American and British allies. Indeed, French desires to call an international monetary conference to "rescue" French involvement in the region fell on deaf ears. The United States never signed the Versailles Treaty and thus never recognized the legality of French "protection" and the direction of policies followed by the successor states. The shock with which the French viewed America tilting in favor of Central Europeans who had been urging revision of the Versailles Treaty is understandable. French ambitions in the region were first challenged by Mussolini's Italy and subsequently by Nazi Germany. Unable to stand on their own, such successor states as Yugoslavia, Czechoslovakia, and Romania were doomed to political and economic disaster.

If Hoover simply lost patience with French pretensions, Roosevelt regarded those he met as frivolous and pedantic, traits for which he had veiled contempt. His well-known disregard for formal doctrines and French insistence on the preservation of the gold standard and fixed exchange rates produced little mutual respect and even less understanding and sympathy toward French efforts on the European continent. It is indeed sad commentary on the statesmanship of the inter-war period. The world was worse off.

NOTES

1. See especially Anna J. Schwartz, "A Review of Explanations of 1929-1933," *Proceedings & Reports of the Center for Yugoslav-American Studies, Research, and Exchanges, Florida State University*, vols. 12-13, ed. George Macesich (Tallahassee: Center for Yugoslav-American Studies, Research, and Exchanges, Florida State University, 1978-1979).

2. See George Macesich, "The Quantity Theory and the Revenue Expenditure Theory in an Open Economy: Canada 1926-58," *The Canadian Journal of Economics and Political Science* (August 1964): 368-90.

3. See, for example, H. W. Arndt, *The Economic Lessons of the Nineteen Thirties* (London: Frank Cass and Co., 1963); Moritz J. Bonn, *The Crumbling of Empire: The Disintegration of World Economy* (London: George Allen and Unwin, 1938); John P. Day, *Introduction to World Economic History Since the Great War* (London: Macmillan and Co., 1939); Milton Friedman and Anna J. Schwartz, *A Monetary History of the U.S., 1867-1960* (Princeton, N.J.: Princeton University Press, 1963); J. K. Galbraith, *The Great Crash* (Boston: Houghton Mifflin, 1972); Claude W. Guillebaud, *The Economic Recovery of Germany, from 1933 to the Incorporation of Austria in March, 1938* (London: Macmillan and Co., 1939); Calvin B. Hoover, *Memories of Capitalism, Communism, and Nazism* (Durham, N.C.: Duke University Press, 1965); Keith Hutchinson, *The Decline and Fall of British Capitalism* (New York: Charles Scribner's Sons, 1950); Alfred E.

Kahn, *Great Britain in the World Economy* (New York: Columbia University Press, 1946); League of Nations, *The Network of World Trade* (Geneva: League of Nations, 1932-1944); League of Nations, *World Economic Survey* (Geneva: League of Nations, 1932-1944); David Meiselman, ed., *Varieties of Monetary Experience* (Chicago: University of Chicago Press, 1970); Bertil Ohlin, *International and Interregional Trade* (Cambridge, Mass.: Harvard University Press, 1935); Arthur C. Pigou, *Aspects of British Economic History, 1918-1925* (New York: Macmillan, 1947); Lawrence Smith, "England's Return to the Gold Standard in 1925," *Journal of Economic and Business History* (February 1932): 228-58; Ingvar Svennilson, *Growth and Stagnation in the European Economy* (Geneva: United Nations Economic Commission for Europe, 1954); David Williams, "London and the 1931 Financial Crisis," *Economic History Review* (April 1963): 512-28; Leland B. Yeager, *International Monetary Relations, Theory, History, and Policy, Part II* (New York: Harper & Row, 1966); Allyn A. Young, "Economics and War," *American Economic Review* (March 1926): 1-13.

4. See, for example, the discussion in Herbert Stein, "Pre-Revolutionary Fiscal Policy: The Regime of Herbert Hoover," drawn from his *The Fiscal Revolution in America* (Chicago, Ill.: University of Chicago Press, 1969).

5. See, for example, the well-known studies by Milton Friedman and David Meiselman and their tests on the stability of money velocity and investment multiplier in the United States; and footnote 2 for Canada: G. Macesich and F. A. Close, "Comparative Stability of Monetary Velocity and the Investment Multiplier for Austria and Yugoslavia," *F.S.U. Slavic Papers* 3 (1969).

6. See, for example, George Macesich, "The Sources of Monetary Disturbances in the United States, 1834-45," *Journal of Economic History* (September 1960): 407-34.

7. Leland B. Yeager, *International Monetary Relations: Theory, History and Policy, Part II* (New York: Harper and Row, 1966) writes "The idea of fixing the value of all moneys in relation to the standard gold coin became common only in the nineteenth century. The full-fledged gold standard arose in Great Britain." (251) He continues, "The international gold standard was a comparatively brief episode in world history. We cannot specify a precise date when it began. It did not exist in 1870 and did exist in 1900. World War I marked its end, for the post war attempts at restoration can hardly be considered successful. The international gold standard was in full sway only from perhaps 1897 to 1914, less than twenty years." (255)

For discussion of the international specie standard before 1860, see George Macesich, "The Source of Monetary Disturbances in the

United States, 1834-45," *Journal of Economic History* (September 1960) and George Macesich, "International Trade and United States Economic Development Revisited," *Journal of Economic History* (September 1961), reprinted in Stanley Cohen and Forest Hill, eds. *American Economic History: Essay in Interpretation* (Philadelphia: J. B. Lippincott, 1966).

> British foreign investments shortly before World War I amounted to roughly twice the French, more than three times the German, and many times as large as the foreign investments of any other country. Probably something over half of the British foreign investment was outside the British Empire, largely in the United States and Latin America. Figures such as these highlight the contrast between Britain's financial leadership in the days of the international gold standard and America's much less dominant position nowadays; they show the special nature of historical circumstances in the international gold standard worked as well as it apparently did. (Yeager, *Monetary Relations*, 256)

8. Yeager notes:

> The system of the 1920's was not merely precarious; it contained seeds of monetary deflation in particular. Whether or not there was an overall shortage of gold—a question much discussed at the time—the existing supply was unevenly distributed. The United States in the early 1920's and France in the late 1920's acquired and kept unduly large shares of the world's gold. Other countries, including England, were in much the same position as if there had been an overall shortage. Their external positions required restrictive policies at home, while countries with relative surpluses of gold were reluctant, for fear of inflation, to pursue the expansionary policies that would have eased the strain of others. For the world economy as a whole, monetary policies were thus bedeviled by a clash, manifesting itself differently in different countries, between domestic and balance-of-payment considerations. Policy could not aim at a single consistent set of objectives. (Yeager, *Monetary Relations*, 292)

9. Little attention appears to have been paid by countries to the "rules" of the gold standard game in the pre- and post-World War I period, though the evidence is far from conclusive. Yeager, *Monetary Relations*, drawing on the work of Arthur I. Bloomfield, *Monetary*

Policy Under the International Gold Standard: 1880-1914 (New York: Federal Reserve Bank of New York, 1959) and Ragnar Nurkse, *International Currency Experience* (Geneva: League of Nations, 1944) write that "over the period 1922 through 1938 the traditional reinforcement of gold flows was the exception rather than the rule." By and large, central banks appeared to be "offsetting" or "neutralizing" the internal effects of gold inflows and outflows. Surprisingly enough, a similar conclusion appears to hold true for the pre-1914 gold standard as well: year-to-year changes in the international and domestic assets of central banks were in opposite directions more often than in the same direction. Yeager, *Monetary Relations*, 288.

Several factors could explain the apparent inconsistency as Yeager (*Monetary Relations*, 288) correctly points out: First, gold flows could have occurred with such a lag as to be concealed in the figures of year-to-year changes; second, the apparent neutralization may have often been "automatic" rather than the result of deliberate policy, with international and domestic assets of central banks tending to move in opposite directions under the influence of the business cycle; third, the inflow of gold, by increasing liquidity of the money markets, could have resulted in repayment of debts to the central bank (and conversely for an outflow); further, passive response to credit demands could have made a central bank's cosmetic and international assets move in opposite directions; fifth, equilibrating capital flows can cushion, or delay, the need for the domestic monetary responses of traditional gold-standard theory.

Another reason may be that supplied by Robert Triffin, *The Evaluation of the International Monetary System: Historical Reappraisal and Historical Perspectives* (Princeton, N.J.: Princeton University Press, 1965, 4) and cited by Yeager is that "as variation in a central bank's domestic portfolio offset only a fraction of any opposite variation in international assets, the latter might still have a multiple impact on the domestic money supply."

Still another reason is provided by Donald N. McCloskey and J. Richard Zecher, "How the International Gold Standard Worked 1880-1913," *The Monetary Approach to the Balance of Payments*, ed. Jacob A. Frenkel and Harry G. Johnson (Toronto: University of Toronto Press, 1976, 357-85). Taking their cue from general equilibrium, they write that the monetary theory approach to the balance of payments implies that "central bankers did not have control over the variables over which they and their historians have believed they had control. The theory assumes that interest rates and prices are determined on world markets, and therefore that the central bank of a small country has little influence over them and the central bank of a large country has influence over them only by way of its influence over the world as a whole." (358) Indeed, they go so far as to maintain:

> It matters little whether or not central banks under the gold
> standard played conscientiously the "rules of the game," that is
> the rule that a deficit in the balance of payments would be
> accompanied by domestic policies to deflate the economy. The
> theory argues that neither gold flows nor domestic deflation
> have effects on prevailing prices, interest rates, and incomes.
> The inconsequentiality of the game may perhaps explain why
> they were ignored by most central bankers in the period of the
> gold standard, in deed if not in words, with no dire effects on
> the stability of the system. (361)

See Gottfried Habler for a review of the Johnson and Frenkel
compilation of studies, *Journal of Economic Literature* (December
1976): 1324-28.

10. In fact, the MacMillan Report issued in Great Britain in June
1931 blamed the instability of the post-war period in part on the fact
that gold movements no longer had their "normal" effect on domestic
policies of certain countries such as the United States and France.

11. "In short, British monetary experience in the 1920's consisted
of: Several years of inflationary struggle back to pre-war parity;
temporary success in this questionable effort; and then continued
business stagnation and chronic unemployment, the need for relatively
high interest rates, and a precarious accumulation of mobile short-
term foreign funds—all under the influence of an inappropriate
exchange rate." (Yeager, *Monetary Relations*, 280)

12. Paul Alpert, *Twentieth Century Economic History of Europe*
(New York: Henry Schuman, 1951); John H. Claghan, "Europe After
the Great Wars, 1816 and 1920, *Economic Journal* (December 1920):
423-35); Theodore E. Gregory, "The Economic Significance of 'Gold
Maldistribution'," *Manchester School of Economics and Social Studies*,
2:2 (1931): 77-80; Theodore E. Gregory, *Gold, Unemployment and
Capitalism* (London: P. S. King and Son, 1933); Theodore E. Gregory,
The Gold Standard and Its Future, 3d ed. (New York: E. P. Dutton and
Co., 1935); Theodore E. Gregory, "Rationalization and Technological
Unemployment," *Economic Journal* (December 1930): 441-67; John M.
Keynes, "The City of London and the Bank of England, August 1914,"
Quarterly Journal of Economics (November 1914): 48-71; John M.
Keynes, *The Economic Consequences of Mr. Churchill* (London:
Leonard and Virginia Woolf, 1925); John M. Keynes, *The Economic
Consequences of the Peace* (London: Macmillan and Co., 1920); John
M. Keynes, "The Economics of War in Germany," *Economic Journal*
(September 1914): 442-52; John M. Keynes, *The End of Laissez-Faire*

(London: Leonard and Virginia Woolf, 1927); John M. Keynes, *Essays in Persuasion* (New York: Harcourt, Brace and Co., 1932); John M. Keynes, "The French Stabilization Law," *Economic Journal* (September 1928): 490-94; John M. Keynes, "The German Transfer Problem," *Economic Journal* (March 1929): 107; John M. Keynes, *A Revision of the Treaty* (London: Macmillan and Co., 1922); John M. Keynes, "War and the Financial System, August 1914," *Economic Journal* (September 1914): 460-86; John M. Keynes with H. D. Henderson, *Can Lloyd George Do It? An Examination of the Liberal Pledge* (London: Nation and Athenaeum, 1919).

13. Stein, *Fiscal Policy*

14. Stephen Roskill, *Hankey: Man of Secrets, Volume II: 1919-1931* (Annapolis, Md.: U.S. Naval Institute Press, 1972): 544.

15. *Ibid.*, 545.

16. A. P. Thornton, *The Imperial Idea and Its Enemies: A Study in British Power* (New York: Auden Books, 1968).

17. William Wisely, *A Tool of Power: The Political History of Money* (New York: John Wiley and Sons, 1977): 174.

18. *Ibid.*

19. See, for example, W. S. Vuchinich, "Interwar Yugoslavia," in *Contemporary Yugoslavia*, ed. W. S. Vuchinich (Berkeley: University of California Press, 1969); George Macesich, "Monetary Policy and International Interdependence in the Great Depression: The U.S. and Yugoslavia," *Zbornik* (Belgrade: Serbian Academy of Sciences and Arts, 1976): 77-100.

20. F. A. Hayek, *Studies in Philosophy, Politics, and Economics* (Chicago: University of Chicago Press, 1967, 348). Also quoted in R. Spencer, "Inflation, Unemployment, and Hayek," *Federal Reserve Board of St. Louis Bulletin* (May 1975): 10. The fact is that statesmen of widely divergent views between the wars distrusted Keynes notwithstanding his brilliance and creativity. See, for example, *The Collected Writings of John Maynard Keynes*, ed. E. Johnson (London: Macmillan; New York: Cambridge University Press for the Royal Economic Society), vol. 17 *Activities 1920-1922: Treaty Revision and Reconstruction*, and vol. 18; *Activities: 1922-1932: The End of Reparations*. See also, the "Review" of this study by Stephen A. Schuker, *Journal of Economic Literature* (March 1980): 124-26. How little Keynes was aware of American institutions and American democracy is suggested in the *Collected Writings of John Maynard Keynes*, ed. Donald Moggridge (New York and London: Cambridge University Press, 1979), vol. 23, *Activities 1940-43: External War Finance*. See also the review of this study by Robert Herren, *Journal of Economic History* (June 1980): 451-52. Herren draws attention to Keynes' lack of understanding of the American scene: "Of particular

interest are Keynes' comments on the decision-making process in the U.S. Keynes was amazed and slightly appalled by the institutional situation in this country [the United States]. He wondered 'how decisions are ever reached' in this country [United States] in such an 'inefficient' system." (106) According to Herren, Keynes "found that all the administration had good intentions toward his plans, but that it could not control Congress. His comments are useful to those scholars who are trying to understand the institutional framework, within which Keynes formulated his prescriptions for economic policy." (452)

21. *Collected Writings*, vols. 17 and 18, and Keynes' *Essays in Persuasion* (New York: Harcourt, Brace and Co., 1932).

22. Schuker, *Review*, 126.

23. Milo Keynes, ed., *Essays on John Maynard Keynes* (New York and London: Cambridge University Press, 1975) and Harry Johnson's contributions, especially pp. 111-21.

3

A Theory of Cooperation

Many of the successor states embarked on the torturous road to democracy have thus far achieved indifferent results—some even catastrophic, for example, in the former Yugoslavia and parts of the former Soviet Union. Thanks to misguided nationalists whose achievements have promoted little more than inter-ethnic strife, the newly minted sovereign states face each other in a mean state of anarchy. Can the various ethnic groups within new sovereign states create reliable cooperative strategies? Can cooperation emerge in a world of sovereign states? In short, can cooperation evolve from non-cooperation? Specifically, how can cooperation get started at all? Can cooperation strategies survive better than their rivals? Which cooperative strategies will do best, and how will they come to predominate?

Many of the problems facing these ethnic groups and nations take the form of an iterated Prisoner's Dilemma.[1] In the Prisoner's Dilemma game, two individuals (ethnic groups or nations) can either cooperate or defect. The payoff to a player is in terms of the effect of the payoff. No matter what the other does, the selfish choice of defection yields a higher payoff than cooperation. But, if both defect, both do worse than if both had cooperated.

To illustrate, let us assume that A (major ethnic group) and B (minor ethnic group) in Table 3.1 agree to trade. Both are satisfied with the amount they will be receiving. Assume further that for some reason the exchange is to take place in secret. Both agree to place money in a designated location. Let us also assume that neither A nor B will ever meet again or have further dealings.

Table 3.1
Prisoner's Dilemma

	Ethnic Groups A	Ethnic Groups B
C Cooperation	R = 3,3 Mutual Cooperation	S = 0,5 Sucker's Payoff
D Defection	T = 5,0 Temptation to Defect	P = 1,1 Punishment for Mutual Defection

Note: A = Major Ethnic Groups; B = Minor Ethnic Groups; the game
          is defined by: $T > R > P > S$ and $R > (S + T)/2$.

Now if both A and B carry out their agreement, both stand to gain.
It is also obvious that if neither A nor B carried out the agreement,
neither would have what it wanted. It is equally obvious that if only
one carried out its end of the bargain, say A, B would receive
something for nothing, since they will never again meet or have
further dealings. Thus, there is an incentive for both A and B to leave
nothing. As a result, neither A nor B get what they initially wanted.
Does the logic prevent cooperation? That is the Prisoner's Dilemma.

The iterated Prisoner's Dilemma can be made more quantitative to
allow study by game theory methods and computer simulation. In
order to do this, we build a payoff matrix presenting hypothetical
values for the various alternatives, such as Table 3.1.

In this matrix mutual cooperation by A and B yields 3 points to
both parties. Mutual defection yields to both 0 points. If A cooperates, but B does not, B gets 5 points because it is better to get
something for nothing. The number 3 is called the reward for
cooperation R. The number 1 is called the punishment or P. The
number 5 is T for temptation, and 0 is S, the sucker's payoff. The
conditions necessary for the matrix to represent a Prisoner's Dilemma
are the following:

$$T > R > S. \tag{3.1}$$

$$T + S < R. \tag{3.2}$$

The first condition (3.1) says that it is better to defect no matter what the other side does. The second condition (3.2) guarantees that if A and B get locked into an out-of-phase alteration, for example, A cooperates but B defects in one period and B cooperates but A defects in the second period, A will not do better. In fact, A will do worse than if A had cooperated in each period.

If A and B will never meet again (an unlikely situation in our example), the only appropriate solution indicated by the game is to defect always. This strategy is correct even though both could do better if they cooperated. Thus, in the case of Prisoner's Dilemma played only once, to defect is always the best strategy.

In the case of our iterated Prisoner's Dilemma game where the same two participants may meet more than once, a much greater set of options is available. Strategy would include a decision rule which determines the probability of cooperation or defection as a formation of the history of interaction thus far. However, if there is a known number of interactions between a pair of individuals, to defect always is still evolutionarily stable (e.g., individuals using the strategy of defection cannot do better by another strategy). The reason is that the defection on the last interaction would be optional for both sides. So too would defection on the next to the last interaction and on back to the first.

On the other hand, if the number of interactions is not fixed in advance, but given by some probability, W, that after the first interaction the same two individuals (ethnic groups/nations) will meet again, other strategies become evolutionarily stable as well. Indeed, when W is sufficiently great, there is no single best strategy regardless of the behavior of the other in the population. The matter, however, is not hopeless.

In fact, Axelrod and Hamilton demonstrate that there is a strategy that is stable, robust, and viable. Accordingly, evolution of cooperation can be conceptualized in terms of three separate questions:

1. *Robustness.* What type of strategy can thrive in a variegated environment composed of others using a wide variety of more or less sophisticated strategies?
2. *Stability.* Under what conditions can such a strategy, once fully established, resist invasion by mutant strategies?
3. *Initial Viability.* Even if a strategy is robust and stable, how can it even get a foothold in an environment which is

predominately noncooperative?[2]

The authors submitted various strategies to a computer tournament drawing upon contributors in game theory from economics, mathematics, political science, and sociology. The result of the tournament was that "the highest average score was attained by the simplest of all strategies submitted: Tit-for-Tat. This strategy is simply one of cooperating on the first move and then doing what the other player did on the preceding move. Thus, Tit-for-Tat is a strategy of cooperation based on reciprocity."[3]

The robustness of Tit-for-Tat is reported by the authors as dependent on three features: "It was never the first to defect, it was provocable into retaliation by a defection of the other, and it was forgiving after just one act of retaliation in the long run, Tit-for-Tat displaced all other rules and went to fixation" and so provides "further evidence that Tit-for-Tat's cooperation based on reciprocity is a robust strategy that can thrive in a variegated environment."[4]

The authors then demonstrate that once Tit-for-Tat has gone to fixation, it can resist invasion by any possible mutant strategy provided that individuals who interact have a sufficiently large probability, W, of meeting again.

Since Tit-for-Tat is not the only strategy that can be evolutionarily stable, it begs the question of how an evolutionary trend to cooperative behavior could ever have started in the first place. Axelrod and Hamilton provide several illustrations where benefits of cooperation can be harvested by groups of closely related individuals.

Clustering can also lead to a Tit-for-Tat strategy even when virtually everyone is using an all D (Defection) strategy. Suppose that a small group of individuals is using Tit-for-Tat and that a certain proportion, p, of the interactions of the members of the cluster are with other members of the cluster. Then the average score attained by members of the cluster using Tit-for-Tat strategy is

$$ p \left[\frac{R}{(1 - w)} \right] + (1 - p) \left[\frac{S + WP}{(1 - w)} \right] \tag{3.3}$$

If the members of the cluster provide a negligible proportion of the interactions for the other individuals, then the score attained by those using all D is still $P/(1 - w)$. When p and w are large enough, a cluster of Tit-for-Tat individuals can then become initially viable in an environment composed overwhelmingly of all D.

Can the reverse happen? That is, once a strategy of Tit-for-Tat becomes established, can it be displaced? According to the authors, the answer is no. This is because the score achieved by the strategy that comes in a cluster is a weighted average of how it does with others of its kind and with the predominant strategy. Each of these components is less than or equal to the score achieved by Tit-for-Tat. Thus the strategy arriving in a cluster cannot intrude on Tit-for-Tat. In other words, when w is large enough to make Tit-for-Tat an evolutionarily stable strategy, it can resist intrusion by any cluster of any other strategy.

In sum, "cooperation based on reciprocity can get started in a predominantly noncooperative world, can thrive in a variegated environment, and can defend itself once fully established. The gear wheels of social evolution have a rachet."[5] It is noteworthy for our purposes that Tit-for-Tat won the various tournament games not because it managed to beat the other players but by eliciting behavior from the other player that allowed both to do well. Indeed, it was so consistent in generating initially rewarding results that it achieved a higher overall score than any other strategy in the tournament.

So-called not nice or tricky strategies designed to sound out how much an opponent "minded" being defected against typically backfired, causing severe breakdowns of trust. In other words, attempts to use defection in a game to "flush out" an opponent's weak spots turns out to be very costly. Indeed, it proved more profitable to have a policy of cooperation as often as possible, together with a willingness to retaliate swiftly in a restrained and forgiving manner.

Furthermore, straightforwardness and simplicity are the best approach. Being incomprehensibly complex is very dangerous indeed because this type of strategy can appear to be chaotic. The use of a random strategy can appear as one that is unresponsive to the other player. An unresponsive strategy provides no incentive for the other player to cooperate.

The significance of these results, for instance, for the ongoing dialogue between major and minor ethnic groups in countries is obvious. It is not surprising that the byzantine strategies followed by some participants in the dialogue have meager concrete results.

Among the important lessons for inter-ethnic and new nations are dialogues derived from Axelrod's tournament efforts revealing that previous game theories did not take their analysis far enough. That is, it is important to minimize echo effects in an environment of mutual power. He argues that a sophisticated analysis calls for going "three levels deep." The first level is the direct effect of a choice. Since a defection always earns more than cooperation; this is easy. The second level is the indirect effect which takes into account that the other side may or may not punish a defection. In the third level, response to the defection of the other side may repeat or even amplify one's own exploitative choice.

Thus a single defection may be successful when considered for its direct effects and perhaps even for its secondary effects. The tertiary effects, however, may be the real costs when one's own single defection turns into unending mutual recriminations. Many of the rules were actually punishing, with the other player simply serving as a mechanism to delay the self-punishment by a few moves.

In essence, there is a lot to be learned about coping in an environment of mutual power. Indeed, Axelrod reports that many expert strategists from economics, political science, mathematics, sociology, and psychology made the systematic error of being too competitive for their own good, not forgiving enough and too pessimistic about the responsiveness of the other side.

In a nonzero sum world, an ethnic group or nation does not have to do better than another player ethnic group or nation to do well for itself. The more player nations interact the better. As long as A does well, it is alright if the others do as well or a little better. It is pointless for A to be envious of the success of another ethnic group or country.

Consider another example from relations between debtor and creditor countries. A country that borrows from another can expect that the loan will be mutually beneficial. There is no point in the borrower's being envious of the creditor's terms and interest. Any attempt to reduce it through an uncooperative practice, such as not making interest and principal payments on time as agreed, will only encourage the creditor to take retaliatory action. Retaliatory action could take many forms, often without being explicitly labeled as punishment. Poorer credit ratings, less prompt deliveries of needed materials, fewer discounts, and, in general, less favorable market conditions for the debtor country's goods and services. In short, the retaliation could make the loan quite expensive. Instead of worrying about the relative profits of the creditor, the debtor should worry about whether another borrowing strategy would be better. For instance, it can lift domestic restrictions on interest paid on savings and bank deposits, thereby mobilizing greater domestic savings which could reduce external borrowing requirements.

The significance of the environment for the endogenous evolution of institutions à la Hayek is in the results reported by Axelrod and others in the ecological tournament.[6] The tournament consists of not only a single subjective replay, but also an entire cascade of hypothetical replays, with each one's environment determined by the preceding replay. In particular, if you take a program's score in a tournament as a measure of its fitness, and if you interpret fitness to mean number of progeny in the next generation, and finally if you let the next generation mean "next" tournament, then the result is that each tournament's results will determine the environment of the next tournament. This type of iterated tournament is called ecological because it stimulates ecological adaptation or the shift of a fixed set of species populations by their mutually defined and dynamically developing environment as contrasted with the mutation-oriented aspects of evolution, where new species can come into existence.

Carrying the ecological tournament generation after generation causes the environment to gradually change. In the beginning, both good and poor programs or strategies are equally represented. As the tournament progresses, the poorer programs drop out while the good ones remain. The rank order of the good ones will now change since the field of competitors has changed.

Success breeds success only if the successful programs are permitted to interact. If, in contrast, the success of some programs is due mostly to their ability to exploit less successful programs, then as these exploit-prone programs are gradually squeezed out, the exploiter's base of support is eroded and it too will bail out. As Axelrod points out, playing with rules that do not score well is eventually self-defeating. Not being nice may look promising at the start, but in the long run, the effect is to destroy the very environment upon which its success depends.

Consider the ongoing circumstances in the newly minted countries against our theory of cooperation outlined above. Cooperation based on reciprocity can gain a foothold through at least two different mechanisms. One is through kinship or closely related individuals or institutions. A second mechanism to overcome a strategy of total defection (all D) is for the mutant strategy (cooperation) to arrive in such a cluster that will provide a nontrivial proportion of the interaction each has. The extensive trade relations which now make for increasing world interdependence provide such a cluster.

As reported by Axelrod and Hamilton, a computer tournament approach will demonstrate that a strategy of Tit-for-Tat will fare better than alternative strategies. It is robust. It does well in a variety of circumstances. It is stable and especially against a wide variety of mutant strategies. Cooperation can indeed prosper. It can emerge in a world of egoists without central control by starting with a cluster of individuals/nations who rely on reciprocity.

In short, advice given to players of the Prisoner's Dilemma might also assist national leaders and others in newly established nations in dealing with the current opportunities before the world: Don't be envious; don't be first to defect; reciprocate both defection and cooperation; and don't be too clever. These guidelines will serve to gauge various proposals cast up to deal with reform and ethnic problems in the following chapters of this book.

Allowances must be made in the application of the Prisoner's Dilemma game to ideology, bureaucratic policies, and quality of leadership. Nevertheless, the insights are very useful. Our process of understanding and approach to problems of cooperation are enhanced by the knowledge that mutual cooperation can emerge without central control by starting with a cluster of units which rely on reciprocity. When it is learned that X will lead to Y and Y is felt to be desirable, there is an inclination not to prevent Y by not prohibiting X. The process of trial and error in dealing with such global issues as reform and ethnic strife is slow and painful. The conditions for cooperation and mutually rewarding strategies based on reciprocity are there.

Our theory of cooperation gives added insight into a problem addressed by Mancur Olson—why institutional sclerosis crept up on the West, but at different speeds in different countries.[7] According to Olson, the explanation is to be found in the politics and economics of common interest groups and collusive associations. Some interest groups strengthen society but others reduce growth, efficiency, and the capacity to adapt to outside events. Such common-interest organizations tend to prevent or delay changes in relative incomes and prices required when productivity changes or the system is subject to an external shock. Unlike price monopoly however, the influence of the group is not even efficiently wielded. In effect, they are cartelized organizations cautious about change and innovations.

The political consequences are perhaps even more important than the strict economic effects. Interest group lobbying increases the scope and complexity of government. This focuses the resources on political lobbying, negotiations, and political activity. Individuals with a talent for such activities will be favored over those with strictly technical, entrepreneurial, and other talents. These collusive organizations are expensive to start. Each member has an incentive to be a "free rider" on the actions of others. Participation is costly in terns of fees, lobbying, and time. To be effective, the leadership of such organizations must make it worthwhile for individuals to participate. This may take the form of pecuniary or nonpecuniary returns, moral pressure, or outright coercion. It takes many years for these incentives, pressures, and loyalties to evolve, but once established, interest groups tend to maintain themselves indefinitely at much less cost.

Cases in point consistent with Olson's hypothesis are Great Britain, which led and promoted the Industrial Revolution and the American industrial heartland. On the other side, there are cases where concerned interest organizations have been eliminated by foreign occupation, totalitarian government, or political instability. According to Olson, these countries experience rapid rates of growth after a free and stable legal order is established. Some examples are the countries of continental Europe in the post-war era.

Eventually many of these common interest organizations were re-established again in Europe. The use of collective and political pressures and collusive organizations once again made it difficult for countries to react to changed market conditions. For example, changed market conditions requiring lower real wages are resisted by workers organized as a cartel or lobby, even though advantageous contracts could in principle be made between employers and unemployed workers. The collusive organizations with the most power to price workers out of jobs are now the labor unions of Western Europe. In America it is more likely that this power is in the hands of various producer groups, including some unions and corporations threatened by imports.

To cast Olson's problem into our theory of cooperation, the discussion of a changing ecological environment must be considerable. Accordingly, the initial success of some of the common interest groups was enhanced by their ability to exploit less successful groups. These groups were eventually squeezed out, and the exploiter's base of support eroded, thereby destroying the very environment for which its success depended. As we noted, not being nice may look promising in the beginning but not in the longrun.

The post-war period in Europe and Japan provides additional insights. The Allies reset the tournament according to a new set of rules. The tournament ran well as long as the game was played with good or nice strategies. As we noted, success breeds success only if nice strategies are permitted to interact. The comparatively better performance of Western European countries and Japan on this score stand in marked contrast to that of the East European countries and the former Soviet Union. In many East European countries, the former common interest groups were replaced, but the expected rapid rates of growth did not always materialize—thanks to misguided nationalist failure to adopt a nice strategy at the outset. By adopting a not nice strategy at once, some of the countries destroyed the environment much more quickly. Even so, reinstitution of a nice strategy with its concomitant positive influence on the environment is still possible in these countries through ethnic, economic, and political reforms which some have undertaken.

NOTES

1. Robert Axelrod and William D. Hamilton, "The Evolution of Cooperation," *Science*, 27 March 1981, pp. 1390-96; Douglas R.

Hofstadter, "Metamagical Themas," *Scientific American*, May 1983, pp. 16-26; Anton Rapoport and A. M. Chammah, *Prisoner's Dilemma* (Ann Arbor: University of Michigan Press, 1965); D. Luce and H. Raiffa, *Games and Decisions* (New York: John Wiley and Sons, 1975), 94-102; M. Cohen, T. Nagel, and T. Scanlon, eds., *War and Moral Responsibility* (Princeton, NJ: Princeton University Press, 1974); B. Belassa and R. Nelson, eds., *Economic Progress, Private Values, and Public Policy: Essays in Honor of William Felnew* (Amsterdam: North-Holland Publishing Co., 1977); M. Taylor, *Anarchy and Cooperation* (New York: John Wiley and Sons, 1976); Robert Axelrod, *Evolution of Cooperation* (New York: Basic Books, 1984); Andrew Schotter, *The Economic Theory of Social Institutions* (Cambridge: Cambridge University Press, 1981); Andrew Schotter and Gerhard Schwodiauer, "Economics and the Theory of Games: A Survey," *Journal of Economic Literature* (June 1980); 479-527; George Macesich, *World Banking and Finance: Cooperation Versus Conflict* (New York: Praeger, 1984).

2. Axelrod and Hamilton, "Evolution of Cooperation," p. 1393.

3. *Ibid.* The strategy of Tit-for-Tat was submitted to the tournament by Professor Anatol Rapoport, a psychologist and philosopher at the University of Toronto.

4. Axelrod and Hamilton, "Evolution of Cooperation," an all D (Defection) strategy.

5. Axelrod and Hamilton, "Evolution of Cooperation," p. 1394.

6. The discussion in the following two paragraphs draws on Douglas R. Hofstadter, "Metamagical Themas," pp. 24-25.

7. Mancur Olson, *The Rise and Decline of Nations* (New Haven, Conn.: Yale University, 1982).

4

The Market Model: A "Nice" Strategy

Thanks to the key role of markets and prices, the market model readily serves to promote Tit-for-Tat "nice" strategy underscored in cooperation theory. The strategy and market model are indeed robust. They do well in a variety of circumstances. They are stable. They can promote cooperation without central control. Prices and markets are the main components of market economies and market democracies. In his book, *Economic Organization*, Frank Knight points out that the economic problem, which is a multiplicity of ends and limitation of means, may be broken down into five interrelated problems.[1]

Provisions must be made by every society for handling these five problems:

1. Fixing standards
2. Organizing production
3. Distributing the product
4. Providing for economic maintenance, and
5. Adjusting consumption to production over short periods.

The existence of alternative ends implies that there must be some way of setting priorities among these ends and resolving conflicting evaluations by individuals within a society. In a free-market economy, this problem is resolved by voting in the marketplace with money. Such an arrangement amounts to proportional representation and allows economic minority groups within a society to make their desires known. These votes in the free-market economy manifest themselves through prices that in turn reflect the standards of society.

When these standards are translated into production in industries, prices are involved again. The task is accomplished by the interaction of two sets of prices: the price of products and the price of resources. The price of products in relation to the cost of production determines the distribution of inputs among industries. The relative price of input factors, in turn, determines the coordination of these factors within industries.

The means to divide the total product must be established by every society. In a society incorporating a free-market economy, this task is accomplished through the price system. Under such an arrangement, separate individuals in a society own the means used in production. They stake a claim on society's product by selling services on the market for a price. An individual's total claim on the product is determined by the quantity of resources he has and the price at which he can sell all the services of these resources. The return per unit of time of resource or input factor prices in conjunction with the distribution of ownership of resources determines the distribution of the total product among individuals and society. In effect, prices serve as signals indicating where economic resources are wanted most and at the same time, produce an incentive for people to obey these signals. Because the function of factor prices is to distribute the product, other prices, mainly product prices, serve to fix standards and organize production. The first three problems described above deal with the adjustment of production to consumption. The organization of existing resources and their utilization are the only economic problems of concern to a static society.

The fourth problem is economic maintenance and progress. In a changing society, however, problems affecting the volume of resources and changes in their utilization require solutions. In a free-market economy, the relevant price for solving this problem is the interest rate, which is an incentive for owners of capital to maintain their capital or to add to it. Where capital is concerned, the individual consumer has a voice in decisions affecting economic growth by his choice of saving.

The fifth problem concerns some provisions that must be made for a quick adjustment of relatively fixed supplies of a commodity to consumption. Bribery, chance, favoritism, or prices are among the means available to society to accomplish this task. When free bidding for goods is permitted, prices adjust so that the quantity people want to buy at the market price is equal to the quantity available.

Prices do three things in solving our five problems:

1. They transmit information effectively and efficiently;
2. They provide an incentive to users of resources to follow such information; and
3. They provide an incentive to owners of resources to follow

this information.

This summary of the role of prices in a free-market economy is a brief and oversimplified version of an extremely subtle and highly complex procedure. The complexities are driven home only when something goes wrong or attempts are made to find substitute methods for solving these five interrelated problems.

THE PRICE SYSTEM AND ECONOMIC DEVELOPMENT

Criticism of the price system on the grounds that it cannot achieve economic development rests on the relevance of external economies and complementarities.[2] According to this argument, private and social benefits differ where economies are external to the firm and the industry. When complementary factors and facilities are lacking, economic development is arrested. Industry, for example, is slow to take advantage of relatively low wages where complementary facilities do not exist.

Although the argument that the price system cannot achieve rapid economic development rests on the existence of external economies, the argument that it will not rests on internal economies and monopoly.[3] For successful operation, the price system requires effective competition as an energy source. Otherwise, the economy rests on dead center with private enterprise and the price system making little economic progress.

There is yet another argument that shows the divergence between private and social costs and the existence of external diseconomies.[4] Accordingly, private individuals may be willing to develop a country's natural resources only if they can appropriate the capital represented by these resources.

In defense of the price system, the advantages most often cited in well-developed economies are in (1) capital formation, (2) dispersal of decisions, (3) risk, and (4) the incentive to innovate.[5] The private entrepreneur usually makes a better collector for capital formation than does the government. Since there is considerable uncertainty about the exact nature of the bottlenecks impeding economic development, it makes little sense to allocate all of one's resources to a single goal, which may be unprofitable in the final analysis. New methods and ideas seldom receive a favorable audience in bureaucracies, where there is a tendency to dodge responsibility and cling to old methods and ideas.

As an economy develops and resources acquire the mobility to allow demand and supply elasticities to become more pronounced, the price system will operate more smoothly; this operation enables marginal and structural changes to occur in the economy. People distrustful of price mechanism operations tend to behave as if they have access to a universal mind and often fail to take advantage of the mechanism's contribution as a delicate integrator of complex economic events. This could cause a serious slowdown in the economy.

Implicit in the "low supply elasticity" argument is the questionable assertion that people in these countries tend to be less aware of alternative opportunities. If so, steps should be taken to improve the market's operation through better information instead of turning to an elaborate planning structure until the elasticities become larger.

Rigid central planners and critics of the price system have overstated their case about external diseconomies and complementarities. For example, in an early work, Ronald H. Coase suggests possible solutions to these vexing problems within the price system.[6] James M. Buchanan's work indicates that imperfections arising from political attempts to solve these problems may outweigh the economic benefits.[7] Viewing the world as though it were composed of complements has serious methodological drawbacks.[8]

MONEY AND THE MONETARY SYSTEM

Nowhere is the need for constraints against undesired outcomes of majoritarian democratic processes more evident than in the exercise of monetary policy. Past monetary policies have been a major cause of economic instability throughout the world. A contributing factor to the poor performance of monetary policy is how easily money slips into the political arena to become a singularly important political issue. Discretionary authority facilitates monetary manipulation for political ends, causing increasing uncertainties about money, the monetary system, and the monetary authority itself. This raises fundamental questions about public policy constraints in the monetary system, the ideas, and economic philosophy underlying past and current monetary policies.

This study considers money and specifically the quantity theory of money within the framework of the organizing principle of a market democracy and market economy. To be successful, a market democracy and a market economy must incorporate a well-implemented and well-executed monetarist rule into monetary arrangements, which will serve to contain money and the monetary system within a defined nondiscretionary and lawful policy system. Money and monetary theory are ideologically neutral. This does not mean that it must be the same in all countries or throughout history, although the evidence put forward by professors Milton Friedman and Anna J. Schwartz supports the view that money does indeed matter.[9] As a result, money is an integral factor in our "nice" strategy.

A MINIMAL POLICY PRESCRIPTION AND ITS CRITICS

The general policy prescription for market economies is that the role of government should be strictly limited, and, in particular, government policy toward business should be minimal. Critics argue that there are limits to this approach. Thus John M. Keynes and his followers argue that market economies can establish macroequilibrium at less than full employment. It is therefore the government's responsibility to bring about appropriate macroeconomic equilibrium. Moreover, given imperfect competition, resource allocation will not be optimal. As a result, government will have to step in to regulate monopoly through its powers of regulation and taxation. Government intervention, critics argue, is all the more necessary to ensure that social and private costs and benefits are considered in private economic decisions.

An important disclaimer to these criticisms is registered by Milton Friedman, and by others who share his views, that the market economy will take care of its monopoly and external problems without government intervention. Government policy failure, rather than market failure, tends to be the rule rather than the exception. An activist government policy is decided primarily by politics rather than by economics. It is far better to rely on the self-correcting forces of a market economy to restore equilibrium than to count on government policy makers to do so.

Critics underscore the issue that a market economy cannot make definitive judgments about equity and how resources should be divided among members of a society. This is an area where only value judgments can be made. We can make the empirical statement that one society may have a more equal income distribution than another. It is equally obvious that how uneven income and wealth distribution are in a society will depend on the distribution of human and physical capital. In turn, this depends on family, inheritance, tax laws, and chance.

Supporters argue that the apparent efficiency of market economies in both the static and dynamic sense compensates for less theoretical control by society over the growth of productive resources. In planned economies, planners can choose higher savings rates, thereby permitting higher investment rates which generate higher economic growth rates than those produced by market economies, where savings and investment rates are a matter of individual choice.

THE UNITED STATES AND OTHER COUNTRIES AS EXAMPLES

In the U.S. economy, resource allocation is determined primarily by market forces, so that presumably a "nice" strategy is followed for the most part. The United States conforms closely to the standard definition of the market model. Of course, there are exceptions to the rule that competition dominates in the United States. Some of the more obvious exceptions are government intervention monopolies and trade unions. Competitive forces, through the exercise of supply and demand, are the principal determinants of resource allocation in the United States.

The role of government in resource allocation in the U.S. economy is an important one. Government activities, such as the regulation and control of industries with market power—albeit difficult to define— have an obvious impact on resource allocation. Still government enterprises in the United States do not command an important share of economic activity, unlike other highly industrialized countries where government's share in industries is significant. Indeed, in the United States more than 75 percent of the economic activity is in private hands.

In the United States, the impact of government on economic activity is primarily through regulation and antitrust policy. For example, the Sherman Antitrust Act (1890) is the principal instrument for regulation and has been given different interpretations by the courts. Moreover, the tax system of the United States does not redistribute as clearly as the tax systems of other countries.

Some people have suggested that in fact traditional American ideology is not as powerful as in the past. For instance, George C. Lodge argues that such American conservatives as former President Ronald Reagan, Senator Barry Goldwater, and former President Gerald Ford represent traditional American ideology that breaks down into five great ideas. These, most closely articulated by John Locke, are as follows:

1. *Individualism.* The atavistic notion that the community is no more than the sum of its parts;
2. *Property rights.* The guarantee that the individual will be free from the predatory powers of the sovereign;
3. *Competition.* The means of controlling the uses of property to serve individual consumer wants;
4. *The limited state.* A government lacking authority to plan

or interfere significantly in economic life but capable of
responding to Crises or interest group pressures;

5. *Scientific specialization and fragmentation.* The theory
that if we attend to the parts, as experts and specialists, the
whole will take care of itself.

According to Lodge, the new American ideology emerging has
quite different elements:

1. *Communitarianism as the replacement to individualism.* If
the community is well designed, its members will have a
sense of identity with it, but if it is poorly designed,
people will be alienated and frustrated;
2. *Rights of membership in the community.* The rights of
survival, income, health, and other basic needs would
replace property rights;
3. *Community needs and purposes.* Substitute for competition
as the method of controlling or justifying the use of
property;
4. *The state as planner.* A setter of community goals;
5. *Holism.* The theory that nature groups units of whatever
kind into wholes and indeed into a single, great unified
whole (i.e., a new sense of crucial interdependency).[10]

While imposing controls and state intervention into the economy
simultaneously, Lodge argues, President Nixon in 1971 affirmed
repeatedly his allegiance to the traditional American ideology of
individualism, private enterprise, competition, and limited government. The plea for free enterprise by business while insisting that the
government come to their defense when threatened with competition
and failure has not gone unnoticed. The government's picking up of
failures instead of serving as a guide simply increases government
intervention. What is lacking, according to Lodge, is economic
planning and the specification of community goals that would
probably reduce the need for government interference in the economy
rather than increase it.

Lodge does not really suggest a cure for American "ills" be
diagnosed; for instance, how is planning to be achieved democratically
if in fact it is to be done at all? He does not advocate government
ownership of large corporations since together with government they
would be stronger than ever. They would, as a result, be even more
unresponsive to the community. This is indeed the case in totalitarian
states. Nor is antitrust action the proper way to preserve and promote
competition and prevent the concentration of economic and political

power.

His suggestion that the 2,000 or so largest corporations receive federal charters leaves open the question of how the government will exercise control without undermining independence and effectiveness. He appears to see Japan as a possible model for how to bring government and business into a more effective relationship but does not take into account the significant cultural differences between Japan and other countries.

Worker participation in management, industrial democracy, or German codetermination provide still other alternatives, though again, these schemes may be difficult for American business and/or labor unions to accommodate. The American political system of two principal parties responds, according to Lodge, to "interest group pluralism." They are therefore incapable of responding to the new communitarian ideology. A new party will likely emerge capable of giving expression to the new ideology. Before this can happen, however, the old American individualism and competitive market economy is in need of infusion with a greater sense of public needs and a better mechanism for planning and action that would be in the public interest rather than in the interests of special groups.

Other countries with working market systems provide additional examples and experiences upon which to draw. For the most part these are the "social market capitalist" countries of the European community. Such member countries as France, Germany, and Italy are functioning market democracies. They differ from the American example in that they resort more to government intervention as a means for redistribution of income and welfare programs rather than as primarily the regulatory function of government intervention in the United States.

Many of the European countries are characterized by extensive and comprehensive social welfare programs involving a higher percentage of total government expenditures than in the United States. In general the influence of government in economic activity and in society is more pervasive than in the United States. Indeed, many of the European countries could perhaps better be described as "communitarian" owing to their reliance on greater government participation.

The European experience may well be more relevant to the successor states in their search for an appropriate model. In terms of cultural and historical factors, the successor states are closer to Europe than to the United States. The "nice" strategy we have discussed is a characteristic of the European model as it is that of the United States insofar as resource allocation is determined primarily by market forces. To be sure, from our cooperative theory, the "nice" strategy tilts in favor of the United States model if individual participants derive more satisfaction from functioning as individuals with greater freedom of choices than as part of a group as underscored in the European communitarian model, where such freedom would be more limited.

NOTES

1. James Buchanan, "Socialism Is Dead: Leviathan Lives," *Wall Street Journal*, 18 July 1990, p. A10.

2. Charles P. Kindleberger, *Economic Development* (New York: McGraw-Hill, 1958), 132.

3. *Ibid.*, 133.

4. *Ibid.*, 133.

5. *Ibid.*, 134.

6. Ronald H. Coase, "The Problem of Social Cost," *Journal of Law and Economics* (October 1960): 1-44.

7. James M. Buchanan, "Politics, Policy and the Pigovian Margins," *Economics* (February 1962): 17-24.

8. George Macesich, "Current Inflation Theory: Consideration of Methodology," *Social Research* (Autumn 1961), pp. 321-30.

9. Milton Friedman and Anna J. Schwartz, *A Monetary History of the United States*, 1867-1960 (Princeton, N.J.: Princeton University Press, 1963); and Milton Friedman and Anna J. Schwartz, *Monetary Trends in the United States and United Kingdom: Their Relation to Revenue, Price, and Interest Rates, 1867-1975* (Chicago: University of Chicago Press, 1982).

10. George C. Lodge, *The New American Ideology* (New York: Alfred A. Knopf, 1975). See also George Macesich, *The International Monetary Economy and the Third World* (New York: Praeger, 1981), 13-17.

5

Economic Systems and Cooperation

In our discussion of the market model and cooperation theory, we underscore five problems which every society must solve. The various institutional arrangements and other means that a society selects to resolve these problems is typically the subject matter of comparative economic systems. Theoretical constructions and comparisons attempt to gauge the impact an economic system may have in providing answers to our fivefold problem. One can argue that the market model facilitates cooperation and the "nice" strategy of Tit-for-Tat. In fact, if it is promoted, cooperation and a Tit-for-Tat "nice" strategy can operate even in a hostile environment such as in "planned socialism" and a single party political system. The difficulty, of course, is that economic systems are influenced by many other factors, including social, economic, geographical, political, ideological, and indeed random.[1] How to control and understand these other factors, while at the same time attempting to gauge the effect of an economic system on economic results, is a formidable task.[2]

Given the multidimensional nature of economic systems, it is useful to consider their characteristics. These include the organization of decision making, whether coordination is determined by market or plan or some combination, property rights, and the incentive system. To facilitate comparison, the literature classifies the various economic systems as pure model systems of capitalism, market socialism, and planned socialism.[3] Thanks to our cooperation theory we can gain useful insights into the various models and their likelihood of success.

The market description and "nice" strategy we have discussed comes close to describing capitalism. Thus, private ownership of factors of production is the key property relationship. The decision making rests with the owners of these factors. These decisions are coordinated by the market which provides the necessary information. Material incentives are used to motivate participants to respond to market signals. The resulting system easily provides scope for the exercise of the Tit-for-Tat "nice" strategy.

Market socialism is usually characterized by public ownership of the factors of production. Decision making is decentralized, and the market mechanism is used as the instrument of coordination. Non-pecuniary and pecuniary incentives are used to motivate participants. The public ownership of resources imposes a constraint on the choice of strategies available to individuals; for example, a "nice" strategy may or may not be selected.

In the case of planned socialism, state ownership of the factors of production is one of the defining characteristics. Another factor is decentralized decision making coordinated by a central plan, which issues rules and standards of behavior to all participants in the system. As in market socialism, both non-pecuniary and pecuniary incentives are used to motivate participants. The scope for the selection of strategies available to individuals is further reduced. The tournament and rules are rigidly set by central outlenders.

Professor Dimitrije Dimitrijević and I have discussed at length the classification of various economic systems, particularly as they relate to the monetary and financial organization.[4] As a practical matter, our conclusion is that if emphasis is placed on the importance of individual freedom, as in market democracies, the threefold classification is useful because it encapsulates the decreasing amount of freedom exercised by economic participants in moving from free-market systems or the increasing freedom as countries move to transform their economies into functioning market democracies.

We should keep firmly in mind that classification of economies is useful but not foolproof. This is also the case with the selection of strategies. As we noted, it is possible for a Tit-for-Tat "nice" strategy to function even in the hostile environment of planned socialism. Most economies are probably best described as resting somewhere between complete freedom to make economic decisions on private property ownership of the means of production, free markets, competition, and full public ownership of the means of production and the ability to command new economic activity.

It is the real world systems populated by mixed economic systems and how they perform that is of interest to policy makers and other observers. Classification that yields abstract models, nevertheless, provides us with a terminology and a "norm" against which actual performance can be judged.

Given that the real world is populated by mixed economies, which incorporate private and public property ownership, markets, planning, non-pecuniary and pecuniary incentives, other complications enter into attempts to gauge how well a particular economic system performs. Thus, in underscoring the importance of the economic system to a country's economic performance, is also its resource endowment. This includes resource endowment, size of the economy, level of economic development, and random events that may well be critical in evaluating performance.[5] In addition, the problem of evaluation is further complicated by the wisdom of policy makers in formulating and implementing a country's policies. This includes the selection of a strategy that enhances cooperation among and between its citizens and national and ethnic groups.

In standard economic analysis, the economic system is taken as a given. The task at hand for analysts in comparing economic systems, however, is that they must gauge the impact of the system and the other factors on the economic outcome. What then are or should be the performance criteria to judge the various systems? Not everyone will agree on the criteria or on their selection. By their nature these decisions are subjective.

Moreover, even if an agreement on the criteria is reached, how then will the weight or degree of importance be assigned to the various outcomes produced by the different systems? Indeed, if some kind of comparison index is desired, then clearly the weight assigned will determine the value of the index, which can be used to gauge the performance of the various systems. Since the weights are subjective, they and the index for comparison will tend to reflect the values of the analyst.

A number of criteria commonly considered for gauging the performance of economic systems include the stability of output, employment, general level of prices, composition of output, individual economic security and employment; economic freedoms of occupational choice, consumption and property; equity, including equality of opportunity—other criteria can be derived from these. Some are complementary, for example, the higher the rate of growth, the greater the level of output in the next period. Others may be in conflict; for example, price stability may be undermined by easy monetary policies designed to raise output.

In sum, the evaluation, comparison, and ranking of economic systems will depend on the performance of the system in regard to the various criteria selected, which are objective and the preference function or functions assigning weights to the several criteria, which are subjective in nature. These systems are also judged by the strategy they select and mount to provide cooperation.

The empirical evolution of comparisons of performance is to first define and quantify the criteria selected, and, second, to carefully and uniformly compare performance with all the attendant difficulties that are involved. These may include differences among countries in the availability, reliability, coverage, and methodology of data. The results produced show the differences in performance, which are then assessed in the light of one or more preference functions. The causes of such differences are subject to the analysis of the nature and operation of the system or systems under review.

To be sure, the comparative economics approach is incomplete in that it is a partial or sectoral view of an economy. A broader view is provided by a comparative systems approach which encompasses the study of an entire economy. In reality, the two approaches are complementary. The partial or sectoral view underscored in the study of economic systems needs a view of the entire system, as in the comparative systems approach.

Thanks to the complexities of comparing systems, it is not surprising that such studies draw on the various disciplines, including philosophy, economics, political science, and other socio-cultural endeavors. Much the same is true when discussing other issues in comparative systems. Certainly the comparative systems approach provides us with more than the parochialism that is inherent in much economic thinking, which tends to draw from the experiences of single systems.

Important too are the character and quality of political groupings and bureaucracies that drive a country's institutions. For example, in democratic societies the powers of the state are exercised by a parliament or congress, a judiciary, and an executive branch, including the bureaucracies. Coalitions of political parties typically mold these relationships. For their part, the political party or parties in power must also come to terms not only with the opposition but also with various policy makers represented in the government bureaucracy and interest groups.

Issues encapsulated in the view that constraints must be placed on the exercise of discretionary authority by vote-maximizing bureaucracies and political elites if democracy is to thrive and prosper have been discussed in earlier works.[6] A democratic market system based on self-interest cannot be entrusted to an unrestrained bureaucracy and political elite. There is considerable doubt that an enlightened elite of bureaucratic managers can realistically be expected to suppress their individual interest for the general interest. According to our cooperation theory, rules that could set the tournament in process and yield cooperation and constrain arbitrary exercise of authority.

IN SEARCH OF GUIDANCE: LOOKING TO MARKET ECONOMIES

Many of the smaller countries coming upon the world scene are arriving with limited experience with modern economies and much less experience with contemporary socio-political policies, including human rights. The shrill demands by nationalists tend to drown out the moderate voices of reform. Indeed, socio-political and economic reforms become hostage to primitive tribalism and demagoguery. As a result, the policy option that is served up in these emerging countries contains an unhealthy dose of high tariffs, high taxes, and extensive state ownership. In effect, it is the essence of the very model that the world is discarding.

This does not mean that the free-market model is trouble free. It would appear that the western market-oriented countries, while moving into the 1990's, are not turning out a brilliant economic performance that will light the path for those countries struggling to make the transition from a state-managed economic system. Is it, after all, that communism's basic criticism of market-oriented economies has been correct all along—namely, that such economies tend to produce chronic unemployment? The criticism is overdone.

Certainly the unemployment rate in the United States in the opening years of the 1990's is greater than expected. It compares poorly with the decade of the 1980's, or with the mid-1970's, when there was a substantial reduction in the number of unemployed as the economy moved into recovery. It appears that the early 1990's register almost 20 percent more unemployed in the U. S. economy than in the low point of the cycle in 1989 and 1990. In fact, during the first sixteen months of recovery in the early 1980's, the number of unemployed declined by 25 percent.

The other industrial countries seem to have turned in a comparable performance. For the same years, Canada's unemployment is about 10 percent, with little prospect for improvement if forecasts are taken seriously. Indeed, Britain, France, and many countries in Europe are mired in a 10 percent rate of unemployment.

These developments have taken the industrialized world by surprise. Ever since the Great Depression, economic analysis and policy in the United States and in Europe have been aimed at preventing just such a state of affairs. The Employment Act of 1946 is explicit in its assertion that it is the continuing policy and responsibility of the federal government to use every means at its disposal to promote maximum employment, production, and purchasing power.

Although it may surprise some people, the American historical record suggests that these goals were achieved before they were formalized by an act of Congress. Thus, for the first thirty years of the twentieth century, the unemployment rate averaged little more than 4 percent, about the same as it was for the twenty-five year period between 1948 and 1973. Thereafter and particularly into the early 1990's, it appears that economic performance leaves much to be desired.

STABILITY IN MARKET ECONOMIES

What can be done to put the U. S. economy back on track? The answer, of course, depends on the authority asked. On one thing they all seem to agree—namely, that many issues need to be addressed. Some argue that bank regulators need to display a more balanced program between surveillance that helps to avoid credit binges and assurances that permit and encourage a growing economy's credit needs. In their view, there is little to be gained and much to be lost by having been negligent earlier about surveillance, with the active support of some politicians, and now to actively take a very tough stand toward bank lending and operations when other policies are trying to encourage U. S. economic expansion. Often authorities take aim at the U. S. budget deficit as a culprit. They suggest that what is needed is a viable and credible program for working the budget deficit down to 1 or 2 percent of the gross domestic product that could be financed without drawing on foreign sources of capital.

Still others argue that there are two related and immediate problems requiring attention because of their singular impact and contribution to the economic paralysis in the industrial world. Both have to do with the general level of prices and, in effect, with inflation. One view holds that American monetary policy should be so managed as to assure stability in the general level of prices. Evidence from at least two periods of American twentieth century experience (1900-1910 and 1922-1929) suggest that good gains in income, output, and employment can be achieved with price level stability. In both periods real output grew at the rate of 4.5 percent per year—far better than the 2.6 percent annual growth rate registered in the 1980-1990 period.

Does this mean that the most desirable objective would be a zero rate of inflation? Not every one agrees on this subject either. Critics of such an objective point to 1991 and 1992, when the general level of prices registered little, if any, change while the unemployment rate grew and general economic activity continued its poor performance.

Instead, these critics suggest not zero inflation but rather 0 rate of rise in the general level of prices low enough so that unease about the future value of money does not dominate the financial decision of businesses and individuals, as it did in the 1970's. And in the Humphrey-Hawkins Act of 1978 (Full Employment and Balanced Growth Act), Congress argues that the nation's price level objective should be "reasonable" price stability, not zero increases.

There is, however, the constraint that a *de facto* system of fixed exchange rates imposes on more expansive American policies designed to influence a more rapid rate of growth of demand for output. Attempts to engineer an expansion may very well upset the foreign exchange markets.

Before September 1992, the European Community (EC) envisioned a *de jure* system of fixed exchanges. As this system operated, it placed all community members into a slow pattern of growth appropriate for Germany as the dominant economy with the key currency. Needless to say, a slow path that is right for Germany does not necessarily fit the situation in other community-member countries. Until September 1992, they had locked themselves into the same pace because a system of fixed exchange rates does not permit economies to adjust to changing circumstances through allowing exchange rates to move. Few of the member countries were willing to stay the German course.

This system of essentially fixed exchange rates has immobilized the management of domestic economic policy. Unable to pursue the expansionist economic polices required to lower its unemployment rate because at the fixed exchange rate its balance of payments would be upset, Britain moved *de facto* to floating the pound. It appears that other member countries may follow Britain's example. France and Italy may well lead the others in moving away from fixed rates.

Critics have long argued that at any moment in time, countries are at different stages of their economic cycles. A lock-step pattern is likely to lead to trouble. Periods of seeming exchange rate and economic stability are interrupted by explosive breakdowns. Critics note that societies attach differing weights to the objectives of economic policy. For example, Germany is as sensitive to rising inflation as the United States is to rising unemployment. The vigor and dynamics of countries also differ. There is ample historical evidence, critics charge, to avoid a regime of fixed exchange rates.

INTEGRATING EUROPEAN ECONOMIES: LIBERAL AND INTERVENTIONIST VIEWS

There is an ongoing debate between two fundamentally different integration concepts for the European economies—perhaps best described as liberal and interventionist. On the one side, the liberal view argues that economic integration should be aimed at the removal of impediments to voluntary and hence mutually beneficial transactions between individuals who live on different sides of a border. There is little need for the creation of an interventionist, supranational institution. In essence, the liberal view of economic integration reduces the role of the state and promotes the international competition of diverse institutional arrangements.

On the other hand, the interventionist position holds that international competition would produce desirable results only if it were not distorted by the legal and institutional differences among countries. Accordingly, states that wish to obtain the maximum gains from international trade must stand ready to cede sufficient sovereignty to supranational bodies, which in turn will harmonize material policies by reviewing distortion to trade. If the harmonization of policies impairs the competitiveness of firms in previously less-regulated countries, economic integration ought to be complemented by a compensatory redistribution of income from richer to poorer members.

It is in this light that the Maastricht Treaty is important. The integration steps underscored in the treaty are modeled along the lines of an interventionist nation-state. It is the end result of a small group of Western European countries that cooperated very closely in political, economic, and military affairs during the cold war period. As it stands in 1992, the treaty does not offer much for European integration that goes beyond Western Europe. In fact, Milton Friedman and others have said repeatedly that a system of fixed exchange rates is simply an inappropriate currency arrangement in the post-World War II world.[7] These arrangements include the Bretton Woods (1944-1971), the Smithsonian Turmoil (1971-1973), the Snake (1972-1979), the European Monetary System (1979-1992), the undirected efforts of the Plaza (1985); and the Louvre Agreements (1987).

Friedman notes that in order to finance German unification, Germany had to shift from being a large capital exporter to mostly other European monetary system members to becoming neutral or even a capital importer. In effect, Germany had to sell less and buy more from other countries. This required that its goods become relatively more expensive to other countries and their goods relatively less expensive to Germany. Such a task can be accomplished through four possible combinations: inflation in Germany, appreciation of the mark, depreciation of foreign currencies relative to the mark, or deflation in other member European Monetary System (EMS) countries.

Since Germany would not inflate, and the fixed exchange rate arrangement of the EMS ruled out changes in the exchange rate, other

EMS members were required to undertake deflation. The other member countries, such as Britain, Italy, France, and Spain, underwent a severe and prolonged recession and high unemployment in order to maintain their pegged exchange rates with the mark. By September 1992, the price for continuing such a policy apparently became too high for Britain and Italy, causing them to pull the peg and allowing their currencies to float. For all practical purposes, the fixed exchange rate experiment of the EMS ended in failure, as did earlier attempts to tie together a large group of countries with independent political systems and independent policies with fixed exchange rates.

A SOUND CURRENCY

Observers note that despite complaints against Germany and the Bundesbank-induced slump, what Europe has been experiencing is desirable disinflation.[8] In a 1992 Europe of no trade barriers and no exchange controls, European economies have become integrated and currencies interchangeable. Until Britain's departure from the EMS in September 1992, no government of the European Community had the sovereign power to boost spending within its borders, for the results would have simply reverberated throughout the community. In effect, the almost thirty years of rapid inflation for the world is coming to an end. *The Economist* notes that governments in the mid-1970's and early 1980's reined back, but not for long, to prevent inflation from declining to the low levels of the early 1990's. The disinflation was not limited to prices of goods or, to a lesser extent, services but to assets, including land and property values. This asset deflation has left people feeling poorer and less willing to spend. Asset deflation had also reduced the willingness of lenders to lend. Thus, banks like to secure their loans against the collateral of assets. If their collateral is falling in value, they need less. All of this is reinforced because people and companies in many countries borrowed heavily in the 1980's. They are more readily disposed to repay their debts rather than to increase them.

The fact of disinflation is, of course, painful and disruptive. For industry, price weakness appears as much a threat to survival as a lack of volume. It may be just as potent in triggering layoffs. For consumers, job insecurity quickly cancels out the happiness of stable prices.

On the other hand, once adaptation does occur, zero inflation, if achieved, is mostly good news. For once, unindexed taxes on capital investment will serve to promote business activity. The cost of capital is lowered by improving bond and stock markets. In fact, historically, economic growth has been consistently higher following low inflation years.

Moreover, experience in many countries suggests that the road to rapid growth begins with sound money. A sound currency is a reliable standard of value. It is fundamental to all economic activities. Such a condition ensures that people will produce, innovate, save, and invest. A sound currency enables the country to attract foreign investment and enables the many other things to take place that are required to ensure a vital and thriving economy. The recent achievements by such Latin American countries as Argentina, Chile, and Mexico are noteworthy. All three countries were once known as the "lands of inflation." In the early 1990's, all three have a sound currency, which is creating a solid, growth-oriented foundation. It is from this foundation that the three countries draw the economic and political strength to attack the daunting social, labor, and capital market problems left from decades of financial instability.

NOTES

1. Asser Lindbeck, *The Political Economy of the New Left: An Outsider's View*, 2d ed. (New York: Harper and Row, 1977), 214.

2. Frederic Pryor, *Property and Industrial Organization in Communist and Capitalist Nations* (Bloomington: Indiana University Press, 1973), 337.

3. Alexander Eckstein, ed., *Comparisons of Economic Systems: Theoretical and Methodological Approaches* (Berkeley: University of California Press, 1971); Paul R. Gregory and Robert C. Stuart, *Comparative Economic Systems*, 3d ed. (Boston: Houghton Mifflin, 1989); P.T.D. Wiles, *Economic Institutions Compared* (New York: Halsted Press, 1977); Andrew Zimbalist and Howard Fuerman, *Comparing Economic Systems: A Political Economic Approach* (New York: Academic Press, 1984).

4. Dimitrije Dimitrijević and George Macesich, *Money and Finance in Contemporary Yugoslavia: A Comparative Analysis* (New York: Praeger, 1984), 1-32; Dimitrije Dimitrijević and George Macesich, *The Money Supply Process: A Comparative Analysis* (New York: Praeger, 1991), 1-39.

5. T. C. Koopmans and J. M. Montias, "On the Description and Comparisons of Economic Systems," in *Comparison of Economic Systems: Theoretical and Methodological Approaches*, ed. Alexander Eckstein (Berkeley: University of California Press, 1971); P. R. Gregory and R. C. Stuart, *Comparative Economic Systems*, 3d ed.

(Boston: Houghton Mifflin, 1985).

6. George Macesich, *Money and Democracy* (New York: Praeger, 1990). The work of Professor Milton Friedman is, of course, helpful to our understanding of these issues.

7. Milton Friedman, "Déjà Vu in Currency Markets," *Wall Street Journal*, 22 September 1992, p. A18.

8. See *The Economist*, 25 July 1992, pp. 15-16.

6

Economic Ideas: Historical and Theoretical Underpinnings

The development of ideas, particularly ideas dealing with the economic sphere of human affairs is fundamental to an understanding of how systems function and indeed on how cooperation is promoted and achieved. In *Reform and Market Democracy* I have discussed at length the development of market democracy, which I take to mean a pluralistic democracy with a free-market society with private property and civil rights which transcend narrow nationalism and where everyone is free to develop. It stands in marked contrast, for instance, to socialism, which is defined as the organization of society in which the means of production of goods and services is not in private hands. It differs from the narrow capitalism of Karl Marx by incorporating more than three hundred years of experience with economic and political reform. Indeed, it is the essence of the "nice" strategy which I discuss in this study and which can serve the successor states in their transformation into market democracies.

EARLY CONTRIBUTIONS

In the closing years of the twentieth century the specter of communism haunting Europe and about which Karl Marx wrote in 1848 and which later writers named the "Red Specter" had turned gray; Europe surged on a wave of democratic, market-oriented reforms. Evidently it pays to cultivate and subscribe to the organizing principle of market democracy and a "nice" strategy.

This should not surprise us. Many contemporary issues of government interaction and competition—as well as economic and political reform—have been set for more than three hundred years by a school of thought that arose to cope with the problems of England in the period of great change following the seventeenth century. The contributions of the thinkers of that era, particularly to economic thought, are notable and deserve serious study. The brief survey presented in this chapter suggests the importance of their contributions to our study of market democracy.[1]

The organizing principle of market democracy, which appears to correspond best to human nature and accommodates humanity's heterogeneity, is the product of more than three hundred years of economic and political thought. John Locke (1632-1704) prepared the way for a scientific study of political economy when he set forth his exposition of a society based on the natural rights of individuals. Among these rights property loomed large; Locke was a philosopher of the middle-class revolution of 1688. He represented the views of men who founded the Bank of England in 1694. The fight against the divine right of kings was won, and a new social order was dominated by the right of individual property. The connection between money and output—important for market democracy—was examined at the beginning of the eighteenth century. In addition to that of John Locke, the most outstanding contribution was made by John Law (1671-1729). In essence, Locke and Law focused on the obvious fact that total monetary receipts must equal total monetary payments. They contended that increases in the quantity of money and the velocity of circulation not only raised prices but expanded output. Their policy prescription was to increase the quantity of money. Their presentation of policies was designed to create a favorable balance of trade.

Richard Cantillon (1697-1734) focused on the processes by which variations in the quantity of money lead to variations in prices and output, thereby providing useful insights into monetary dynamics. He also recognized what others would later point out—that the nominal quantity of money is beneficial to trade only during the period in which it is actually increasing. Once a new equilibrium is reached, output will return to its original level at a higher price level. This process of increasing the quantity of money, however, cannot last indefinitely because the process leads to an adverse balance of payments and an outflow of money. How to buy the benefits of the inflationary process without generating balance-of-payment problems is a familiar issue in contemporary society.[2]

In the 1760's David Hume (1711-1776) linked the general level of prices to the quantity of money in the now classic theory of money and the theory of the price-specie flow mechanism of international trade. The larger the supply of money, argued Hume, the higher the price level was likely to rise; higher prices, in turn, tended to make exports less competitive in foreign markets and imports more competitive in home markets. A drive to enlarge the supply of money would be self-defeating because the accumulation of specie (gold and silver) would produce effects that would later erode the favorable balance of trade. Moreover, attempts to check such deterioration in the balance of trade by controls of one kind or another would be damaging to the national interest. It would deprive the country of the benefits of international specialization and division of labor.[3]

Henry Thornton (1760-1815), in *An Inquiry into the Nature and Effects of the Paper Credit of Great Britain 1802*, dealt with the same general topic Hume had treated in his monetary policy theories. However, Thornton considered not gold and silver but bank credit, by which he meant bank notes. These were the main circulating medium of value in Britain in his time.[4]

England was the center and testing ground for many of the ideas put forward by economists. In economic theory (as distinct from economic policy), the classical doctrine steadily won its way, especially in the United States, although it had essentially the same character as English commerce. As we will see, continental European preoccupations with economic strategy, misgivings about the moral consequences of the enterprise, historical criticism of economic institutions, and socialist theories of more equitable distribution and more humanistic production did not provide a fertile ground for English ideas.

Indeed, Walter Bagehot (1826-1877) of *The Economist* put it well when he was driven to explain the "obvious reasons why English political economy should thus be unpopular out of England." His explanation has two parts: In effect, it is difficult for most people to understand that political economy is an abstract science; moreover, it is particularly difficult for those whose economic development is less developed and more remote from the assumptions of a political economy than the English.[5]

Although they were rigorous and complete within the assumptions of their theory, many English writers excluded important aspects of economic policy that had been clearly revealed in earlier thought and that have never ceased to be influential in practice.[6] In addition, they did not make allowances for ethical considerations or the complexities of international politics. For them, social policy—particularly the welfare of general workers—although not ignored, did not represent any special problems to society. The controversial issues of past and contemporary economic policy arose largely from these ethical, political, and social factors.

Certainly, by the second half of the nineteenth century concern focused on the economic, social, and political problems cast up by rapidly industrializing European and American societies. Early in the twentieth century, most of the elements of the interventionist economic position, which John M. Keynes articulated later in theory, were in practice. How revolutionary the Keynesian revolution was in this is suggested in the brief survey presented in this chapter.

CLASSICAL CONTRIBUTIONS

The moral dilemma between individual and social benefits, which social philosophers and moralists wrestled with, was resolved by Adam Smith in his analysis of the market economy. His system of natural liberty, free markets, free men, and competition lead to an orderly increase in wealth of the nation. The free competitive play of individual selfishness was shown by Smith to be the source of economic growth, social order, and general welfare. In his view, individualism does not lead to chaos but to order and prosperity.

Smith did more. In *The Wealth of Nations* (1776), he provided economics with an analytical framework. The ideas is of a competitive, self-adjusting market equilibrium following a path of growth and affluence. At the same time, *The Wealth of Nations* was a philosophical treatise concerned with fundamental problems of order and chaos in human society. Smith provided what came to be, especially in England and the United States, the orthodox approach to economic problems and policy—one that is very much alive in the twentieth century.

Critics note two limitations to Smith's analysis of the free market. One is the distribution of income, which, if highly unequal, will signal the market to provide more for the rich and little for the poor. If the distribution of income is wrong, production also will be wrong, however efficiently the market works to produce the goods and services. It is this very problem, in fact, that the early socialists raised and that Karl Marx (1818–1883) later developed into a theory about the breakdown of capitalism.

The second criticism, which is closely related to the issue of economic justice, concerns private property in land and capital. Smith's support for the institution of private property, as both natural and necessary to the preservation of economic incentives, is good liberal doctrine. The fact is, however, that he supports it only in advanced societies. In primitive societies, only labor is considered a factor of production to be rewarded by wages. Conversely, in advanced societies rent on land and profit on capital are also part of the costs of production. Since rent and profit as costs of production are really the products of social organization, not natural phenomena like human labor and the self-interest motive, Smith's idea of an equilibrium of natural forces in the market is compromised.[7]

These shortfalls provide socialists and others with an opening to argue that only a return to labor is natural. Accordingly, only when the full value of output is gained by labor through social ownership of the means of production (land and capital) would the natural state of society be regained. Economic justice would be served because the entire product of society would go to its producers, and society's demand would not be distorted by unearned income.

Thomas R. Malthus (1766-1834), David Ricardo (1772-1823), Jeremy Bentham (1748-1832), and Jean Baptiste Say (1767-1832) contributed enormously to the body of ideas now called classical economics. Writing at the close of the eighteenth century and during the turbulent early years of the nineteenth century, they promoted economics to a "science." These were the years of political, social, and technological revolutions that wiped away the vestiges of feudalism and the old aristocratic order. Much was expected of the American and French revolutions by English intellectuals and others. Some attribute the success of the American Revolution to the support of English liberals. Political reform in England was at the time a pressing issue; even the French Revolution was looked upon favorably because it would bring democracy to France and peace to both countries.

The disappointment was great when the wars with France began and continued for almost two decades. The Napoleonic period dashed all hopes for liberal political reforms in England. The establishment concerned itself with holding the line and rooting out the "radicals." In 1795 the Habeas Corpus Act was suspended for five years; in 1799 the Anti-Combination Laws, which prohibited any combination of workers or employers, were instituted to regulate employment conditions. For the most part these laws were directed and enforced more against labor than against management; suppression ruled these turbulent years.

Nevertheless, problems created by the rapid changes brought about by the war years demanded attention. The most obvious problem concerned the growing number of poor displaced by the economic, political, and social turmoil of the period. This occurred because of demobilization following the Napoleonic wars, and the enclosures of common land, which displaced many farmers from their small plots. These factors only served to promote the growth of cities that were already overburdened with the problems of poverty. Reaction against the French Revolution made it certain that the problems of the poor would receive little priority from conservative policy makers, particularly if solutions required political and social reforms. Still, something had to be done.

A solution was presented by a religious minister, Thomas Robert Malthus. His solution was consistent with the preservation of the status quo and called for minimal government intervention. Government, argued Malthus, can do little in any case because the problem of the poor is moral. The problem has its origins in two propositions: the food supply and the sexual proclivities of man. The result is the Malthusian principle that "the power of population is infinitely greater than the power in the earth to produce subsistence for man."[8]

In effect, "misery and vice" hold population in check. If the supply of food increases, there is a corresponding increase in population until the food supply is brought back to subsistence level, which will stop the population increase. Wages tend toward the subsistence level, which is the natural wage. Any increase in wages above the natural or subsistence level causes the population to grow and wages to decline. If, on the other hand, the price of food increases, wages would be forced up to maintain the subsistence wage. Moreover, increasing relief to the poor would mean taking resources out of the hands of those willing to invest, thus decreasing output.

The implications for the poor are ominous. Relief payment simply raises the wages of the poor above subsistence and results in more people. No increase in food production takes place as poverty continues unabated. This is not a very happy state of affairs, but one for which the government and the conservative establishment are not to blame. Nature must be allowed to take its course.

For David Ricardo, capital accumulation is the mainspring of growth. Economic policy should be directed toward facilitating and promoting such accumulations. His model is based on the belief that economic freedom leads to maximum profits, the source of investment capital, and—in a competitive economy—profit-maximizing investments. Business is to be encouraged because it leads to maximum economic growth.

The political and social issues in England following the Napoleonic wars pivoted on whether the country should become more heavily industrialized or should preserve a balance with agriculture. The issues involved the role of England's landed aristocracy in the country's social and political system. The contest was drawn in Parliament on the so-called Corn Laws and the import of grain into England. Existing laws protected English agriculture against foreign competition without simultaneous significant increases in food prices.

As a result of war-created increases in demand for agricultural products, English farmers enjoyed considerable prosperity. When peace finally came, the farmers and landed interests pushed for the enforcement of the Corn Laws to preserve their prosperity. All sorts of schemes were advanced to promote agriculture as England's leading industry.

All of this was anathema to the English business community as it witnessed high food prices and high wages, reduced profits, and decreased exports—which spelled general ruin for England's industry. In turn, it demanded nothing less than the repeal of the Corn Laws. Ricardo and other economists entered the debate on the side of business interests and against those of agriculture. Ricardo argued that the landowners, not the farmers, benefit if the price of wheat is raised by tariffs. The high price of wheat enables an extension of the land under cultivation, which would not normally be profitable. However, the result in the older wheat-growing areas would be that landowners would raise rents to take advantage of the higher prices received by farmers. Consequently, a larger proportion of the nation's income would go to the landowners, who would use these additional resources not for productive investment but for luxury expenditures.

Moreover, additional capital and labor would be drawn from industry to enlarge agricultural production stimulated by artificially high food prices. The net result would be to distort the nation's productive pattern, retarding the country's natural development of industry. Ricardo noted that high food prices would require high wages and thus high costs of production in industry. Since England must sell the products of industry throughout the world, higher costs would reduce business for English exports and so reduce the level of output of industry. Profits would be reduced, thereby slowing capital accumulation and economic growth from a lack of incentive and investment resources.

If left alone, a country's economy will achieve the maximum growth possible, according to Ricardo. It is, therefore, important that business be left alone to pursue profits; thus, the nation would maximize the amount of savings and capital accumulation that are so necessary for growth. Government intervention would simply make the process of saving and accumulation all the more difficult. In effect, Ricardo reinforced the theoretical and ideological under-pinnings set in place by Adam Smith. Business interests are indeed well served by Ricardo's analysis.

The facility with which the international economy is integrated into Ricardo's model served to reduce all economic phenomena to fundamental relationships among factors of production. It demonstrates that the international division and specialization of labor is advantageous to all nations and that protection of domestic producers serves simply to damage the country imposing such protection. Free trade is beneficial internationally as well as domestically. The famous law of comparative advantage is used in support of the free trade doctrine. Moreover, capital will seek out countries where the returns are highest, provided such nations assure political stability and offer protection for private property rights. All of this remains very much a part of contemporary international trade theory, if not practice.

The realization of the full benefits of free international trade helped to forge a sound international monetary and financial system. Ricardo insisted that the domestic monetary system be regulated to minimize any disruption in the international division of labor. He adopted a "bullionist" position, arguing that the domestic money supply should be directly tied to the country's gold supply. Such an arrangement guarantees that a country suffering from a loss of gold through an unfavorable balance of trade automatically contracts its paper note issue. Contraction in the money supply tends to depress the country's general level of prices; this, in turn, encourages the desired adjustment in international accounts. The deficit country's exports become more attractive to foreigners while imports compete less successfully in home markets as the price of home-produced items declines. Ricardo, in effect, set out the essentials of the classical theory of the gold standard.

The idea that money used as a standard of value consists of bank notes redeemable in specie or bullion and that coins circulate at their value as bullion is central to the body of classical monetary ideas. This money is assumed to be convertible into gold or silver bars and to be freely exchangeable either as coin or as bullion between countries. Its value is fixed at its bullion value, and the rate of exchange between two currencies is easily calculated by comparing the intrinsic value of the precious metals, which would automatically adjust to the "needs of trade" in each country.

Moreover, there is nothing that governments can do about this. If they issued paper money beyond the amount that the public would accept in the belief that these notes could at any moment be converted into gold, the surplus issue would be cashed and the government would have to redeem it with gold and silver from its reserves. If the notes were made inconvertible, their values would fall and the price of gold—indeed, of all commodities—as measured in the paper money, would rise in proportion to their overissue. This was Ricardo's argument in his pamphlet *The High Rise of Bullion: A Proof of the Depreciation of Bank Notes* (1810).[9]

The conclusion drawn by classical theorists is that governments must accept that the only true money (gold and silver, or specie) is beyond their control. All the elaborate government devices for increasing national supplies of specie are self-defeating. Money accommodates itself to the "needs of trade." If governments issue inferior monetary substitutes, their value will depreciate. There is no place, therefore, in classical theory for discretionary, interventionist monetary policies designed to maintain full employment, and balance-of-payments equilibrium or to combat inflation or depression.

It remained to be demonstrated that a free market would also achieve full employment of all resources, including labor and capital. This appears to be demonstrated by Jean Baptiste Say (1767-1832) in his *Treatise on Political Economy* (1803). The principle is Say's Law of Markets. According to Say, there can never be a general deficiency of demand or a glut of commodities throughout the economy. While there may be given sectors or industries in which overproduction may occur (along with a shortage in others), this is only a temporary situation. The fall in prices in one area and their rise in other areas will provide incentives for businessmen to shift production and thereby correct the situation.

Say pointed out that people produce in order to exchange their products for other products. Production thus creates its own demand. In general, it is therefore impossible for production to outrun demand. Say's Law of Markets dominated economic thought on the level of economic activity until the concept was challenged by John M. Keynes in the 1930's.[10]

Jeremy Bentham (1748-1832) and "philosophical radicals" such as James Mill, David Ricardo, and John Stuart Mill agitated for political reform, democratic government, and majority rule. The utilitarian political philosophy that dominated the radicals' thinking called for nothing less than a social system based upon full democratic participation and majority rule. According to Bentham and his utilitarian followers, this was the only way that a social system could maximize its total welfare and distribute it as widely as possible.

Bentham differed significantly from the classical liberalism of the eighteenth century that emphasized individual freedom as the goal of public policy. He saw potential conflict in the idea that only individual action can create welfare. It is possible that the action of one person in pursuit of his own interest may injure another and so reduce his welfare. After all, argued Bentham, human society is organized by man-made institutional arrangements. Conscious action can create social reforms that enable men to live better. In effect, classical liberalism establishes through Benthamite utilitarianism a place for interventionist liberalism emphasizing social welfare. It is intervention and reform justified in terms of individual and social welfare and the "greatest good for the greatest number."[11]

Thanks to Benthamite ideas, economics could henceforth easily incorporate the most laissez-faire individualist as well as the most thoroughgoing social reformer.[12] The analytical apparatus is the same for both. Important differences arise from the assumptions and conclusions that each reaches. This is an attribute that economists preserve to the present time.

All was not well in the post-Napoleonic world. The French Revolution did not bring forth "liberty, equality, and fraternity," nor did the rapid economic and technological advance, usually called the Industrial Revolution, abolish poverty. Indeed, the post-Napoleonic reaction and repression and the re-establishment of old political, social, and economic privileges served to increase poverty and arrest democratic advances for the general public. Critics seized upon the observed inequalities to push from theory to practice an alternative vision of society based on the cooperative element in man's nature, rather than the materialistic profit motive of private capitalism, and egalitarianism in place of the unequal distribution of income that prevailed at the time. To these early social critics, society was an organic whole composed of classes, rather than independent individuals, as held by classical economists. The roots of modern socialism can be found in the post-Napoleonic Europe nurtured by reaction against the economic and political circumstances of the era.

Private property and private ownership of the means of production, argued the socialists, constituted the root cause of the failure of the two great revolutions to abolish poverty and to create a political order of full democracy. A few owners of capital benefitted from these social and technological revolutions, but the majority of people remained mired in poverty. The socialists called for the abolishment of private property and privilege as a first step toward a new society of greater opportunity and dignity for all people.

The humanitarian and idealistic roots of early socialism are typified in the work and writings of Robert Owen (1771-1858). His attempts in England and the United States to establish cooperative communities characterized by commonly owned land and worker-owned enterprises (where profit was not permitted) were not particularly successful. This is not surprising; individualism dominated the era.[13]

Unlike the utopian reformers, Karl Marx (1818-1883) coupled scholarship with revolutionary agitation. It was not enough, according to Marx, to theorize; one must build a revolutionary party capable of seizing power when capitalism collapses. He did not suffer lightly other socialists who happened to disagree with his views. In fact, he established the practice of vitriolic denunciation of opposing views that burdens so much of contemporary socialist literature.

In Marx's view, capitalism, which is a term he invented, is doomed. His demonstration of its demise drew upon the so-called laws of motion of capitalist society. On one level Marx based his argument on the inherent injustices of capitalism that lead ultimately to economic and social conditions that cannot be maintained. At another level his argument was sociological in that class conflict between increasingly affluent capitalists and an increasingly miserable working class will erupt into social revolution. At still another level, the argument is economic with the accumulation of capital in private hands, and the creation and increase of abundance; these factors also lead to the inevitable breakdown of capitalism. At all three levels the idea of conflict is underscored: conflict between the ideal and reality, the moral issue; conflict between labor and capital, the sociological issue; conflict between growth and stagnation, the economic issue. Since this conflict generates change, capitalism, according to Marx, must eventually give way to another social system to replace conflicts and restore ethical, social, and economic harmony. This change is the "dialectical process" whereby socialism will replace capitalism. Thus, Marx created one of the world's most powerful ideologies, whose vision of abundance, equality, and freedom still stands as a challenge to classical-liberal individualism, to private property, and to private enterprise. In effect, it is a challenge to market democracy.[14]

NEOCLASSICAL CONTRIBUTIONS

The rise of socialism, the demand for social justice, and Marx's use of instruments of the dominant ideology to attack its legitimacy (e.g., the labor theory of value and the theory of capital accumulation) prompted a search for a theoretical defense of the existing system. In part, the new defense was that of the philosophy of the individual developed and cultivated by dominant business and economic interests from the mid-nineteenth century through World War II. In effect, it is a reinforced version of the laissez-faire argument discussed earlier in this chapter.

Economists did not take the extreme position of individualism very seriously. For one thing, Benthamite utilitarianism suggested that government intervention may be justified by the "greatest good" argument. For another, economists concerned themselves with pressing social issues for which the philosophy of extreme individualism provided little insight. This did not mean, however, that economists rejected the individual philosophy. On the contrary, they remained within its general framework.

More important, economists intentionally or otherwise developed a new theoretical apparatus that presumably served to refute the Marxian critique of capitalism. This was the neoclassical economics developed after 1870. In effect, the foundation of economics was reduced to the desires and wants of the individual, and the entire theoretical explanation of production, distribution, and prices was based on the single assumption of rational, individual self-interest. Neoclassical economics represented a significant scientific advance; it reduces to the simple but elegant idea of marginalism as a complex set of theories of value, distribution, and return to factors of production. The value of a product or service was seen not as the result of the amount of labor embodied in it, but as the result of the usefulness of the last unit purchased. With marginalism, a new approach to economics developed.

Carl Menger (1840-1921), William Stanley Jevons (1835-1882), Leon Walras (1837-1910), and Alfred Marshall (1842-1924) shifted the focus of economics from social classes and their economic interests (which had been underscored by David Ricardo and Karl Marx) to that of the individual.[15] The individual consumer became central to the theoretical apparatus of economics, which displaced the principle of income distribution envisioned by Ricardo as the mainspring of economic progress and the basis for Marx's theory of the breakdown of capitalism. The system of free markets does maximize individual welfare. Because consumers are assumed to maximize their satisfaction and because production responds to consumer wants, it follows that the result will be welfare maximizing. Moreover, marginalism also shows that the costs of production are pushed to the lowest level possible by competition. If allowed to operate without constraints, the entire economy becomes a pleasure-maximizing machine in which the difference between consumer benefits and production costs is increased to the highest level possible. In short, economics is transformed into a service consistent with the individualist social philosophy of Herbert Spencer and William Summer Graham.

The development served also to reinforce, at least in the United States, the legal theories of U.S. Supreme Court Justice Stephen Field (1816-1899) and the philosophy of unrestricted individualism in U.S. constitutional law. One result of Field's interpretation was the elimination of much state legislation dealing with economic affairs, including the regulation of hours of work, child labor, and factory condition. Private property was thus viewed as a natural right that no government could interfere with lightly.[16]

Marx's challenge was also taken up in the application of marginal analysis to income distribution, which demonstrated that all factors of production—labor and land—earn a wage exactly equal to their contribution to the value of output. Called the theory of marginal productivity, which is based on the last marginal unit, its conclusion is that workers would be paid a wage equal to the last unit of output they produced. The same idea was applied to profits earned from capital and to rent from land. In effect, to each factor of production the same law applied. No one could exploit anyone else because everyone received what he deserved. The entire product was exhausted, and no surplus value existed. Marx's concerns were simply irrelevant.

This happy state of affairs, critics are quick to point out, depends very much on the assumptions of the marginal productivity theory:

1. The theory rests on the assumption of perfect competition.
2. All factors of production must be completely substitutable for one another.
3. There must be no change in costs of production per unit of output as the level of production falls or rises.

Not all economists are satisfied by such assumptions. Indeed, some economists have never accepted the theory of marginal productivity, which they view as singularly unreal. It is the issue of periodic booms and depressions plaguing the rapidly industrializing countries that has attracted considerable public and government attention. During the first half of the nineteenth century, little concern was shown by most economists—thanks to their acceptance of the general propositions of Say's Law of Markets, which states that there should be no periodic economic breakdowns, and the economy should continue to operate at uninterrupted high levels of output and employment. In Say's Law the demand is created by production, and in the aggregate the two can never get out of phase with one another. Economists interested in business cycles typically sought causes outside the framework of production and distribution.

For instance, Stanley Jevons (1835-1882) developed a quantitative relationship between sunspots and business fluctuations. He argued that these fluctuations were connected with variations in the weather patterns affecting all of the earth, probably arising from increased waves of heat received from the sun at ten-year intervals. This simply serves to reinforce Say's Law, because the cause is outside the system of production and distribution. Perhaps the best interpretation within Say's Law is provided by the argument that the monetary system generates instability while the basic system of production and distribution remains stable. If the monetary and financial system is stable, general economic stability is assured.

In 1873 Walter Bagehot (in his now classic treatise on money and finance, *Lombard Street*) spelled out how it was to be done: Limit the expansion of credit to legitimate needs of business through effective action by the "central bank." This would prevent excessive credit issue from overstimulating the economy and thereby developing into a crisis. Once the situation got out of hand, the central bank could probably moderate the crisis, but the economy would simply have to weather the storm.[17]

These theoretical advances served to firmly entrench capitalism and to defend it from its critics. The basic analysis of classical economics was supplemented by marginal utility, marginal productivity, and the monetary theory of business cycles. The free-enterprise economy was pictured as operating to produce what consumers want, thus maximizing welfare by distributing products justly and by normally operating at full utilization of resources. The issue of laissez-faire in neoclassical economics was not a rigidly held doctrine. In fact, the major area of exception was monetary policy, which was assigned to the government and its agent, the central bank. It was their responsibility to preserve economic stability by properly managing the money supply to serve the legitimate needs of business. The banking school influence in the form of the real bills doctrine is obvious here. Even so, such monetary intervention was to be held to a minimum and was to be strictly guided by the free market. In short, discretionary monetary policy was to be limited by the requirements of the free market and within the constraints imposed upon it by the gold standard. As a result, the scope was very limited for the exercise of discretionary authority by central banks.

Arguments raised in support of the mercantile, or banking school, tradition were based on two principal ideas, which economists call the "real bills" doctrine:

1. The country's bank money will expand only in proportion to the needs of trade if banks restrict themselves to discounting only real bills of exchange; the converse will prevail when trade declines.
2. A country's currency will have a desirable elasticity only if commercial banks will maintain a reasonable liquid reserve position and will operate competitively.

The first idea, which stressed the limiting effect of quality on the quantity of loans, prevailed in the United States and elsewhere prior to 1860. Thereafter, the quest for elasticity and liquidity dominated the banking scene.

Although the rationale of the real bills doctrine has been attacked throughout history by economists and others, it has never been completely vanquished. Indeed, the doctrine is firmly lodged in central and commercial banking practices. Supporters of the doctrine argue that it provides an intrinsic, self-regulating limit to the quantity of bank money. It provided the chief support for banking reform in the United States before 1913; the Federal Reserve Board embraced it thereafter. While the doctrine can be found in various qualitative control measures over bank credit, it also influences the preferences of central banks for interest rates and money market conditions as policy targets over monetary magnitudes.

Neoclassical economists also approved of other types of government intervention. Such intervention served to facilitate the operation of free competition and free markets. On this score, concern with monopolies and legislation designed to control their practices tended to be supported by most economists. The fact is that neoclassical economics does not adopt lock, stock, and barrel the simple individualism and laissez-faire policies, as critics assert; neither does it opt for wholesale intervention. It does accommodate the realistic needs of society. It does have strong ideological implications because it serves to rebuild the theory of free, private enterprise on a new basis, thereby making the refutation of Marx unnecessary. Private property and free, private enterprise weathered the Marxist storm more or less intact, thanks to the efforts of neoclassical economists.

PHILOSOPHY OF THE WELFARE STATE

These issues, however, were not settled to the satisfaction of all concerned. At the close of the nineteenth century, a continuing concern about the complex nature of man and his society simply had not been adequately addressed—either by those who argued that society is the arm of individual units, brought into an easy equilibrium by market forces, or by those who argued that the social system is divided into antagonistic classes with social conflict fueling change. There was yet another view, one arguing that the chief objective of society is to promote human welfare; it was, in effect, the philosophy of the welfare state. Its exponents included such diverse entities as Roman Catholic popes, Fabian socialists, New Deal proponents, and Great Society advocates.

Papal economics attempted to come to terms with the social problems bubbling up from European industrialization and nationalism, which brought a new socioeconomic and political order to the continent during the last quarter of the nineteenth century. Pope Leo XIII (1910–1903) issued a series of encyclicals between 1871 and 1901, opting for the middle ground in the feud between labor and capital. The problem, argued Pope Leo, was not economic but moral. The solution must be based on justice animated by charity. Because these are nonmarket phenomena, they cannot be measured by the market-place parameters of profit-loss and wages-costs.

The papal tilt was at first toward capitalism in the condemnation of socialism and the defense of private property. Subsequently, a compromise evolved in an indictment of laissez-faire policies (*On Conditions of Labor*), condemnation of socialism, and support for private property rights and the natural rights of individuals. Harking back to the theories of Thomas Aquinas in the thirteenth century, the papal appeal criticized the extreme individualism of the market economy and called for a return to human and community values.

Papal economics asserted that government intervention is justified whenever the welfare and preservation of society is threatened. In these matters, justice and fairness are to serve as guides. The tradition established by Pope Leo continued to influence later popes, Roman Catholic labor movements, and some political parties. The idea that man and community are one, along with an emphasis on and reconcili-ation of both individual freedoms and individual welfare in a society that stresses community values and social justice, continues to be attractive.

For instance, Pope John Paul II's encyclical, written during the summer of 1981, was intended to be a sequel to the encyclicals of Pope Leo XIII (*Rerum Novarum*, 1891) and Pope Pius XI (*Quadragesimo Anno*, 1931).[18] Both are powerful social documents, and the new encyclical of John Paul II is a comprehensive statement on social issues. It backs labor unions, urges worker participation in manage-ment, and proposes a "just" family wage and subsidies that would free mothers from the necessity of taking jobs. The encyclical condemns both "rigid" capitalism and the "collectivist system" that eliminates all private ownership of the means of production. It suggests a socialist middle ground as a model for economic development. The central theme in the 99-page, 22,000-word encyclical (*Laborer Exercens—On Human Work*) opposes the "dehumanizing excesses" of modern economic systems.

The encyclical, written in Polish, reflects John Paul's vision of "a just society based on an ideal economic system." John Paul strongly endorses the workers' right to organize unions, to participate to some extent in the management of their companies, and to strike, except for political purposes or in essential public services. Radical and urgent changes are necessary to rescue farmers from the big landowners and "to restore to agriculture their just value as the basis for a healthy economy." Multinational corporations are engaged in the condemnable practice of fixing high prices for their products while trying to keep down prices for raw materials and semi-manufactured goods, thereby widening the gap between rich and poor nations. "In order to achieve social justice in various parts of the world, there is a need for new movement of the workers and with the workers," according to Pope John Paul. It is sure to be studied carefully in the successor states of the former Soviet Union, the Pope's native Poland, and in Latin America, as well as in other countries where the Roman Catholic church is influential.[19]

While the papists grappled with the social, economic, and political chaos in Europe brought about by an industrial society, Fabian socialists John A. Hobson and Richard H. Tawney in England promoted ideas and programs to deal with similar concerns. Essentially interventionist, their ideas cast government's role as one that assists man in developing his talents to the utmost. This was to be done by government's working to remove barriers in man's path to the "good life."

A cascade of social legislation descended upon England as a result. Legislation dealing with factory safety became law in 1891 and 1895; limiting working hours for women and children in 1891; slum clearance in 1890; increased powers for labor unions in the 1890-1900 period; workmen's compensation and child welfare in 1906; old age pensions in 1908; town planning and redevelopment in 1909; sickness and disability insurance in 1911. While serving as mainstays to contemporary economies, many articles of welfare legislation were put into place by the turn of the century.

Even though their vision is behind much English social legislation, generators and spokesmen of unorthodox ideas such as John Hobson received little gratitude from significant numbers of their contemporaries. In fact, Hobson could not find employment in English universities. However, his writings—*Work and Wealth Incentives in the New Industrial Order*, *Physiology of Industry*, and *Evaluation of Modern Capitalism and Imperialism*—fortunately did much better.[20] Indeed, V. I. Lenin (1870-1924) incorporated into communist ideology Hobson's *Imperialism*, which attacked the selfish expansion of European states.

Like Hobson, Fabian socialists envisioned a society with the highest moral standards through a democratic socialist regime designed to promote as much happiness as possible, for the largest possible number. A small but influential intellectual group included such members as George Bernard Shaw, Sidney and Beatrice Webb, H. G. Wells, and Annie Besant. Named after the Roman general Fabius Maximus, "the delayed," who fought Hannibal with guerrilla tactics instead of frontal confrontation, the name signifies the society's philosophy and plan of action. Their vehicle, *Fabian Essays*, established in 1889 under the editorial leadership of Shaw, promoted the gradual extension of state intervention in economic affairs to improve working conditions, to replace monopoly with government ownership, and to promote a more egalitarian distribution of income.[21]

Unlike the Marxists, the Fabians did not view the state as an instrument of class warfare that must be destroyed; rather, it was seen as a means of social control that, once seized, could be used to promote social welfare. In 1906 they pushed successfully for the formation of a labor party with a socialist platform. Their tactics involved political action within the framework of democratic, parliamentary government. In short, resort to persuasion rather than revolution was a singular Fabian characteristic. That these efforts bore fruit is indicated by the existence of the British Labor party and much of contemporary social and welfare legislation in Great Britain.

Drawing on world experience, the economic historian Richard Tawney (1880–1963) argued for a society reformed along the functional lines of a socialist society. Rewards are to be received by those productive members of society who expend work and effort in the tasks society requires, not to such unproductive elements as the promoter, speculator, and rentier who collect large sums of unearned income. Property rights, according to Tawney in *The Acquisition Society* (1920), should not be maintained if no service is performed. In *Religion and the Rise of Capitalism* (1926), he debated the issue raised by Werner Sonbart and Max Weber over whether the Protestant Reformation created the intellectual atmosphere that made possible the rise of modern capitalism. He argued that the two are related, but also that modern society and its business activities are completely amoral. In *Equality* (1931), Tawney's theme is that egalitarianism can support and sustain a democratic political framework. It is through socialism that human values can receive their necessary development.[22]

The American approach to these same problems of industrialism is characteristically pragmatic, lacking much of the socialist philosophy prevailing in Great Britain and Europe. Workable solutions to specific problems are sought within the traditional framework of American society. Much of the necessary work is attributed to a small group of economists investigating such issues as business cycles, labor relations, monopoly, big business, and social welfare. Through their influence on progressive political leaders at the turn of the century and, later, the New Deal, the theme was promoted that modern industrial society faced serious problems that would not solve themselves. Government intervention was necessary if the destructive forces of the free market were not to have singularly tragic results for both society and the individual.

Thorstein Veblen (1857–1929) represents one of the more important economists through his influence on American reform thought. Essentially, his argument is that the fundamental forces of change are at work to require adaptations of the social, economic, and political institutions inevitably opposed by the establishment and represented by wealth and influence. He sees conflict between change and vested interests. His critique of the "pecuniary society" and the "business system" gave both direction and viewpoint to the movement for economic and social reform. Veblen's two books, *The Theory of the Leisure Class* (1899) and *The Theory of Business Enterprise* (1904), are considered economics classics.[23]

John R. Commons (1862-1945) and his followers formulated specific reform measures and legislation that were adopted first by some states and later incorporated into the New Deal platform of F. D. Roosevelt. Programs and policies such as utility regulation, collective bargaining, and mediation to settle disputes between labor and management on a voluntary basis, along with unemployment insurance and workers' compensation, and the promotion of economic growth, employment, and stability, are cases in point—clearly a remarkable achievement.

According to Commons, the government must serve as a mediator between conflicting economic interests and between economic forces and the individual. He does not necessarily reject the Marxist view of class conflict. In fact, he goes beyond both of them to argue that the market can reconcile some but not all of the conflicting interests that arise in a modern economy. In such an economy, continual conflicts emerge which require government intervention to obtain equitable solutions.[24]

The New Deal philosophy in essence owes much to Veblen, Commons, and their followers. Through government intervention, the public is protected from the worse consequences of an industrial, market-oriented society. The philosophy represents a singular shift from the view of a harmonious, self-regulating, free-enterprise, market-oriented economy, as advocated by the classical and neoclassical economists.

The New Deal administration's intervention into the economy followed three paths:

1. Use of the federal budget to promote adequate aggregate spending in the economy to offset shortfalls in the private sector of the economy. It recognized government responsibility for economic stability in the economy. This recognition is now embodied in the Employment Act of 1946 and is institutionalized in the Council of Economic Advisors to the President.
2. Attempts to promote cooperation between businessmen and

    labor in various industries.
3.   Government intervention into regional land-use planning
    based on water resources (e.g., the Tennessee Valley
    Authority).

According to the liberal reform philosophy of the New Deal (and in contrast to classical and to present-day liberal views), the individual does not necessarily contribute most to society by pursuing his own interest, nor is he necessarily responsible for all of his misfortune. Therefore, society must accept responsibility for the welfare of each individual to enable him to function effectively in society. The passage of welfare measures such as unemployment insurance, workers' compensation, social security, and federal grants-in-aid in health and education are aimed at providing security for the individual.

In addition, businessmen are to accept social responsibility beyond mere profitmaking. The pre-New Deal situation whereby businessmen ran roughshod over human and social values is no longer tolerated. In short, business must justify itself by something more than profit. What that "something" is, however, is not specified. All of this does not serve to endear the reform liberals to the business community.

The liberal reform philosophy of the New Deal extended into President Truman's Fair Deal and, afterwards, into the short-lived administration of President Kennedy. It was picked up in the Great Society programs of President Johnson and was essentially carried on through the administrations of presidents Eisenhower, Nixon, Ford, and Carter. What appears to be a resurgence of neoliberalism and neoclassical economics through "supply-side" economics in President Reagan's administration received considerable attention in the 1980's. The fact is that reform liberalism, as manifested in the past several U.S. presidential administrations, managed to restructure much of the country's economic and social framework without gross violations of individualism, private property rights, and the market-oriented private enterprise economy.

Events took a less satisfactory course in Russia and in Eastern European countries during and after the two world wars. War, revolution, and counterrevolution served to wreck what appeared to be promising liberal reforms, which began at the turn of the century and continued, although at a halting pace, into World War I.

At the time, Russia was the most backward country in Europe, with a primitive system of agriculture and an industry staffed by an illiterate population. By professing its allegiance to a Marxist ideology, which postulated that socialism would naturally evolve into highly industrialized economies for the working-class majority, Russia was at odds with received socialist doctrine. The country simply did not square with what Karl Marx and his followers had in mind. To complicate matters, the world revolution had failed, and the new Soviet state was surrounded by antagonistic capitalist countries who considered it an "illegitimate child of history."

V. I. Lenin (1870–1924) led the Bolshevik Revolution to a successful conclusion. He did so after convincing his followers that Russia could bypass the capitalist industrial era and move directly from an agricultural, semi-feudal society into an era of socialism. Lenin formulated the basic ideas on how to accomplish the goal of a socialist society, which meant that the large-scale industrialization of Russia would be the vehicle to build a working-class society to nurture socialism. This required an alliance between workers and peasants under a workers' dictatorship, although priority was given to the construction of an urban and industrial society; however, Lenin died before his strategy was translated into a specific program of action. A debate on goals and means continued in the 1920's and 1930's until Joseph Stalin ended discussion with the first of the purge trials that were to shake the very foundations of the new Soviet state.

Stalin (1879–1953) manipulated the great urbanization/industrialization debate to his favor. The moderates—led by the leading Marxist theoretician, Nikolai Bukharin—argued for balanced economic development and postponement of world revolution until the Soviet state was strong enough domestically to support such a revolution successfully. Although urbanization and industrialization were to be encouraged, it was dangerous for the Soviet state to push the peasants too far and to threaten their loyalty to the regime any further. In short, a slower development pace tuned to the realistic possibilities of the Soviet state was prudent. Stalin called this approach the "right deviation."

Opposing the moderates was the so-called left wing of the Communist party led by Leon Trotsky (1879–1940), who, in fact, was Lenin's key man during the Bolshevik Revolution. The idea promoted by the left wing called for mobilizing the country's economy to the utmost, squeezing living standards in order to free resources for industrial development, and using the power of materials and export. According to their view, agriculture was to be collectivized and mechanized. In effect, the economy was to be deliberately unbalanced in order to force industrialization. As for the international scene, the Soviet state would never be secure in a capitalist world. As a result, it could best protect itself by exporting world revolution principally by demonstrating the superior productivity of socialism through economic growth.

At first, Stalin took the position of supporting rapid industrialization and the forced draft development advocated by the left wing, but he ruled against collectivization of agriculture to avoid alienating the peasants. As for world revolution, he sided with the moderates and Bukharin to form an alliance, which drove Trotsky into exile. Thereupon Stalin sided with the left and opted for collectivization of agriculture, a rapid rate for the accumulation of capital beyond anything called for by Trotsky and his faction. This move also gained Stalin the support necessary to purge Bukharin. In essence, the debate resolved itself into the establishment of ambitious development goals and a planning apparatus to carry them out, with the Stalin dictatorship as the driving force behind it.

This became the modified Soviet model, which was imposed in Eastern European countries following World War II. It is also the model and system dropped by Josip Broz Tito (1892–1980) in Yugoslavia following the Tito-Stalin split in 1948. With Yugoslavia's escape to pursue its own, independent road to socialism through its unique model of "worker self-management," a new chapter in socialism began; the world would never be the same. The collapse of various socialist countries in the 1990's and subsequent reforms are testimony that the road is indeed a dead end.

With a post-World War I Europe and the Bolshevik Revolution as background, one can gain useful insight into the efforts by John M. Keynes to formulate new policies designed to preserve and revitalize the market economies of Europe. To Keynes, the challenge was clear enough. The Marxist-Leninist socialists had engineered a revolution that not only brushed aside everything before it but transformed a backward, rural economy into an industrial giant. Already weakened by war, European civilization was by now threatened with extinction.[25]

At the time, against apparent socialist success, Britain continued its deflationary policy designed to achieve international stability at the expense of internal stability, as it had in the post-Napoleonic years. Keynes argued that Britain's return to the gold standard at the British pound's pre-war par would diminish British exports and would cause domestic wages, prices, employment, and output to fail. Keynes argued for a managed monetary system to replace the classic gold standard. His advice was disregarded, and Britain returned to the gold standard—only to realize the validity of his prophecy. Already crippled by war, the dissolution of its empire, and economic stagnation, Britain joined the rest of Europe to wait for a miracle. In Keynes' view, Europe could not afford to wait.[26]

This was Keynes's vision, although he lacked the theoretical apparatus to convince an audience educated in classical and neoclassical economics. To demonstrate the futility of the British government's deflationary monetary policy, he had to show the inadequacy of the classical theoretical apparatus, which rested on the relationship among the gold standard, the domestic level of employment, and Say's Law of Markets. Keynes realized the need to demonstrate convincingly the relationship between the theory of employment and monetary theory. He devoted more than a decade to the task.

The two-volume *Treatise on Money*, published in 1930, was Keynes' first effort to unravel the problem. Essentially, he argued the distinction between investment and savings and their different underlying motivations. Unlike Say's Law, which holds that the two must be equal, Keynes argued that this need not be the case. For instance, if savings are greater than investment, general economic activity will decline. Conversely, Keynes' policy prescription, which he argues in the various *Essays in Persuasion*, is similar in the *Treatise*: The monetary system should be managed to assist in maintaining equality between savings and investment in order to promote economic stability. In addition, a program of public works should be put in place to reduce the undesirable effects of economic depression on employment.[27]

As we discussed earlier, the collapse of the world economy and the onset of the Great Depression of the 1930's created a political and economic environment that was receptive to the new ideas advanced by Keynes and others. Contributions to economics made by members of the National Bureau of Research, the University of Stockholm (the Swedish School)—including such economists as Knut Wicksell (1851-1926), D. H. Robertson, William T. Foster, W. Catchings, and others—paved the way for acceptance of Keynes' ideas, now presented in his *General Theory of Employment, Interest, and Money* (1936). The principles are essentially those he put forward in the *Treatise*. The new development in *General Theory* is the concept of equilibrium at less than full employment. Accordingly, an equilibrium is possible at a depression level; however, unless a change takes place in the relevant variables, the economy will stagnate indefinitely. These ideas stood in direct opposition to the classical and neoclassical theories dominating economic thought and practice for more than a hundred years.

For practical politicians in search of theoretical justifications for deficit financing already under way in many industrial countries, the *General Theory* came at the right time.[28] It provided a theoretical foundation to the commonsense view that large government expenditures financed by borrowing were needed to ease the hardships of the depression on the population. It appeared to recognize the advantages of a self-adjusting market mechanism, which was argued so eloquently by classical and neoclassical economists, although its important assumption that wages and prices are determined externally to the system was at odds with received theory. This was important, for it reinforced the theory's basic interventionist position. It called for government to manage the general level of economic activity in the interests of society in a manner consistent with individual freedom and a stable social order. In effect, Keynesian economics provides and articulates the theoretical framework for the reform—liberal policies promoted in the United States, Great Britain, and elsewhere since the beginning of the twentieth century. Keynes thus manages to give coherence to his vision and to socioeconomic and political changes accelerated by the tragedies of World War I and the collapse of the world economy in the post-war years.

Correct or not, Keynes offers a politically attractive alternative to received theories and policies, which appeared to be detached from reality. This does not mean that other explanations are not consistent with the evidence. I have discussed these explanations elsewhere and will again call attention to a number of them in later chapters of this study.[29]

NOTES

1. In the mountain of literature on the evolution of ideas, see Ellis T. Powell, *The Evolution of the Money Market, 1385-1915* (London: Frank Cass, 1966); Warren J. Samuels, "Adam Smith and the Economy as a System of Power," *Review of Social Economy* (October 1973): 123-37; L. Rogin, *The Meaning and Validity of Economic Theory* (New York: Harper and Row, 1938); J. J. Spengler and W. R. Allen, *Essays in Economic Thought* (Chicago: Rand McNally, 1960); George Stigler, *Production and Distribution Theories* (New York: Macmillan, 1941); J. Dorfman, *The Economic Mind in American Civilization*, vol. 3 (New York: Viking Press, 1949); E. K. Hunt, *History of Economic Thought: A Critical Perspective* (Belmont, Calif.: Wadsworth, 1979); Carl Menger, *Problems of Economics and Sociology* (Urbana: University of Illinois, 1963); J. A. Schumpeter, *History of Economic Analysis* (New York: Oxford University Press, 1954); Ludwig von Mises, *The Anti-Capitalistic Mentality* (New York: Van Nostrand, 1956); E. J. Hamilton, A. Rees, and H. G. Johnson, eds., *Landmarks in Political Economy*: selections from the Journal of Political Economy (Chicago, University of Chicago, 1962); Frank H. Knight, *The Ethics of Competition* (New York: Augustus M. Kelley, 1950); E. Whitaker, *Schools and Streams of Economic Thought* (Chicago: Rand McNally, 1961); J. Viner, *Studies in the Theory of International Trade* (New

York: Harper and Bros., 1937); D. Vickers, *Studies in the Theory of Money* (Philadelphia: Chilton Co., 1959).

2. In some of the early writers, we see anticipations of theories advanced much later. See, for example, Thomas Joplin (1790-1847); Thomas Attwood (1783-1856); Nicholas Barbor (1640—1698); William Lowndes (1652-1724); Bishop George Berkeley (1658-1783); John Locke (1632-1704); Richard Cantillon (1697-1734), *Essai sur la nature du commerce en général 1730-1734*; and John Law (1671-1729). D. Vickers, *Studies in the Theory of Money, 1690-1776* (Philadelphia: Chilton Co., 1959), makes the point that there was more Keynesian-type economics in the early period than has often been recognized.

3. See David Hume (1671-1729), "Of Interest; Of Money" in *Essays, Moral, Political, and Literary*, vol. 1 of *Essays and Treatises* (Edinburgh: Bell and Bradfute, Cadell, and Davis, 1804).

4. For example, Anna J. Schwartz, *A Century of British Market Interest Rates 1874-1975* (London: The City University, 1981), writes that Henry Thornton (1760-1815), who in his *Enquiry into the Nature and Effects of the Paper Credit of Great Britain* (1802) expressed concern about the British monetary system during the Napoleonic era, understood

> the fallacy of the real-bills doctrine; the distinction between the first round and ultimate effects of monetary change; the lag in effect of monetary change; the problem market participants faced in distinguishing relative from general price changes; the distinction between internal and external gold drains; the factors influencing the foreign exchanges including the role of purchasing power parity; how to bring inflation under control; the relation of the Bank of England to other English banks; types of effects of monetary disturbances on interest rates; the distinction between the market rate and the natural rate of interest and between nominal and real rates of interest. (1)

See also the interesting exchange between Jacob A. Frenkel and Charles R. Nelson in their article, "On Money," on whether David Hume believed in a stable long-run Phillips Curve: Charles R. Nelson, "Adjustment Lags versus Information Lags: A Test of Alternative Explanations of the Phillips Curve Phenomenon," *Journal of Money, Credit, and Banking* (February 1981): 1-11; Jacob A. Frenkel, "Adjustment Lags versus Information Lags: A 'Comment' and 'Reply' by Charles R. Nelson," *Journal of Money, Credit, and Banking* (November 1981): 490-96.

5. See Walter Bagehot (1826-1877) in his classic on money and

finance, *Lombard Street* (1873). Reprint (New York: Arno Press, 1969).

6. See J. J. Spengler, *Origins of Economic Thought and Justice* (Carbondale and Edwardsville: Southern Illinois University, 1980) for a useful review of the early contributions of economic thought as well as a bibliography.

7. Adam Smith, *The Wealth of Nations* (1776, London). Reprint, 2 vols. ed. R. H. Campbell, A. S. Skinner, and W. B. Todd (Oxford: Clarendon Press, 1976).

8. Thomas R. Malthus, *Essay on the Principle of Population as It Affects the Future Improvement of Society* (1798). Reprint, with Introduction by M. Blaug (Homewood, Ill.: Richard D. Irwin, 1963).

9. David Ricardo, *The High Rise of Bullion: A Proof of the Depreciation of Bank Notes* (1810). Reprinted in *Works and Correspondence of David Ricardo*, ed. P. Sraffa, Vol. III (Cambridge: Cambridge University Press, 1951; New York: Cambridge University Press, 1973).

10. Jean Baptiste Say, *Treatise on Political Economy* (1803).

11. Jeremy Bentham, in his classical works on political reform, democratic government, and majority rule.

12. George Tabalas, "Some Initial Formulations of the Monetary Growth-Rate Rule," *History of Political Economy* (Winter 1977): 525-47, writes, "Even more significantly, early formulations of Friedman's rule span backward to the writings of Jeremy Bentham [1748-1832] and Henry Thornton [1750-1815] at the start of the nineteenth century and to the neglected writings of John Gray, during the 1830's and 1840's." (p. 536)

13. Robert Owen, whose reform efforts included attempts to establish cooperative communities with land owned in common and worker-owned enterprises.

14. Karl Marx, *Das Kapital* (1948, originally published in 1867-1895).

15. Carl Menger, William Stanley Jevons, Leon Walras, and Alfred Marshall, *Principles of Economics* (London: Macmillan, 1930).

16. Stephen Field, United States Supreme Court Justice.

17. Walter Bagehot, *Lombard Street* (1873).

18. Pope Leo XIII, *Rerum Novarum [On Conditions of Labor]*, 1891), which was the Magna Carta of labor; and Pope Pius XI, *Quadragesimo Anno* (1931).

19. Pope John Paul II, *Laborem Exercens [On Human Work]*, 1981).

20. John Hobson, *Work and Wealth Incentives in the New Industrial Order* (1921); *Physiology of Industry* 1956); and *Evolution of Modern Capitalism and Imperialism* (1926).

21. G. B. Shaw, ed., *Fabian Essays* (1789).
22. Richard Tawney, *Acquisitive Society* (1920); *Religion and the Rise of Capitalism* (1926), and *Equality* (1931).
23. Thorstein Veblen wrote two economics classics: *The Theory of the Leisure Class* (1899) and *The Theory of Business Enterprise* (1904).
24. John R. Commons, *The Economics of Collective Action* (New York: Macmillan, 1950).
25. John Maynard Keynes, *General Theory of Employment, Interest, and Money* (New York: Harcourt, Brace, and Co., 1936); and *Treatise on Money* (1930).
26. It is useful here to quote John M. Keynes, "A Short View of Russia," in *Essays in Persuasion* (New York: Harcourt, Brace, 1932):

On the economic side I cannot perceive that Russian Communism has made any contribution to our economic problems of intellectual interest or scientific value. I do not think that it contains, or is likely to contain, any piece of useful economic technique which we could not apply, if we chose, with equal or greater success in a society which retained all the marks, I will not say of nineteenth century individualistic capitalism, but of British bourgeois ideals. Theoretically, at least, I do not believe that there is any economic improvement for which Revolution is a necessary instrument. On the other hand, we have everything to lose by the methods of violent change.

In Western industrial conditions, the tactics of the Red Revolution would throw the whole population into a pit of poverty and death.

But as a religion, what are its forces? Perhaps they are considerable. The exultation of the common man is a dogma which has caught the multitude before now. *Any* religion and the bond which unites co-religionists have power against the egotistic atomism of the irreligious.

The modern capitalism is absolutely irreligious, without internal union, without much public spirit, often, though not always, a mere congeries of possessors and pursuers. Such a system has to be immensely, not merely moderately, successful to survive. In the nineteenth century it was in a certain sense idealistic; at any rate, it was a united and self-confident system. It was not only immensely successful, but held out hopes of a continuing crescendo of prospective success. Today it is only moderately successful. If irreligious Capitalism is ultimately to defeat religious Communism, it is not enough that it should be economically more efficient—it must be many times as efficient. (306-7)

27. John Maynard Keynes, *Treatise on Money* (1930).

28. See also the interesting discussion in W. R. Allen, "Irving Fisher, FDR, and the Great Depression," *History of Political Economy* (Winter 1977): 560-87. John Kenneth Galbraith writes, in "Came the Revolution" (Review of Keynes' *General Theory*), *New York Times Book Review*, 16 May 1965:

> By common, if not yet quite universal agreement, the Keynesian revolution was one of the great modern accomplishments in social design. It brought Marxism in the advanced countries to a halt. It led to a level of economic performance that now inspires bitter-end conservationists to panegyrics of unexampled banality. For a long while, to be known as an active Keynesian was to invite the wrath of those who equate social advance with subversion. Those concerned developed a habit of reticence. As a furtive consequence, the history of the revolution is, perhaps, the worst-told story of our era. (34)

Useful on this score are sections of the four essays published by *The Economist* to commemorate the century of J. M. Keynes' birth: Milton Friedman, "A Monetarist Reflects," *The Economist*, 4 June 1983, pp. 17-19; F. A. Hayek, "The Austrian Critique," *The Economist*, 11 June 1983, pp. 39-41; Paul Samuelson, "Sympathy from the Other Cambridge," *The Economist*, 25 June 1983, pp. 19-21; John Hicks, "A Skeptical Follower," *The Economist*, 18 June 1983, pp. 17-19.

29. See George Macesich, *The International Monetary Economy and the Third World* (New York: Praeger, 1981); George Macesich, *The Politics of Monetarism: Its Historical and Institutional Development* (Totowa, N.J.: Rowman and Allanheld, 1984).

7

Bureaucracy and Market Democracy: Barriers to a "Nice" Strategy

Our discussion suggests the extent to which the exercise of market democracy has been modified by interventionist ideas. Certainly, experience with the Industrial Revolution and its upheaval and later events had much to do with the promotion of these ideas from theory to practice. One consequence of the practice of interventionist ideas was increased authority of the state and its bureaucratic apparatus. This expansion was expedient but inglorious, necessary but dangerous, useful but costly. Along with the expansion came growing concern over the ability of the public to deal on equal terms with the maximizing behavior of an "artful and ever active" bureaucracy and political elite. Experience confirms that constraints must be placed on the exercise of discretionary authority by vote-maximizing bureaucrats and political elites if market democracy is to thrive and prosper.[1] Cooperation theory provides insights on how the task of organizing and implementing constraints can be accomplished.

The public must insist that such constraints be put in place. Indeed, it was that shrewd observer of American democracy, Alexis de Tocqueville, who warned in the first half of the nineteenth century that democracy could falter as a consequence of citizens' diminished interest in restraining central authority.[2] He noted that because democratic man would not be able to count on his neighbors for support, he had an incentive to increase the power of the central authority.

Even earlier, the American founders—for instance, James Madison—were aware that their project, the federal constitution, was an exercise in constructing government out of defective human parts. They believed that the urge to tyrannize others was so strong that external restraints became absolutely indispensable. The image of man in their discourse appears less than free and rational because his will and intelligence may be at the service of his "passions," forces beyond himself that make self-control improbable. In both the Federalist and anti-Federalist political factions, a vague egalitarianism also led to the fear of elitism—"the artful and now active aristocracy" usurping the power that belonged to an unalert and passive people, as Walter Lippmann succinctly put it when he informed Americans that the framers of the Constitution had bequeathed to future generations of Americans a government of checks and balances.

Certainly the task of constraining the bureaucracy and political elite is made all the more difficult by utopian attempts to make the uncertain certain by control of society according to plan. Monetary policy, albeit important, is but a case in point. Monetary uncertainty originating primarily from fluctuations in the purchasing power of money will tend to move the social order away from the use of money and markets toward a greater reliance on some form of greater government control or command organization, thereby strengthening bureaucracy and its political influence. Moreover, monetary instability and market failure are closely linked and both serve to weaken the social fabric.

Another illustration, which will serve bureaucracy, is the rise of socialism in the 1930's, which promoted central economic planning and the redistribution of income policies. The Keynesian Revolution stressed the failure of the economic system, which was avoidable by the application of scientific knowledge. Harry Johnson is surely correct when he writes that these two movements reinforced one another.[3] In turn, this led to the view that economic backwardness can be traced to defects in the private enterprise system and market democracy, not to the backwardness of people and their cultures in relation to the requirements of modern industrial society. Since then, the Third World has promoted this view to the top of the worldwide development agenda through demands for a new international economic order (NIEO).[4]

THE STATE AND BUREAUCRACY

Rapid socio-political and economic change, particularly since the Great Depression, has brought with it a growing bureaucratic influence as well as increased demands for reform to constrain bureaucracy's taste for discretionary authority. This urgency is underscored by growing evidence from the experience of the former socialist countries of Eastern Europe. The violations of public trust and confidence by domestic bureaucracies in those countries are now common knowledge.

The fact is, however, that a government and its bureaucracy do not operate in a vacuum. They are products of previous and present values and beliefs about what government should do and how it should be done. Modern bureaucracy is the result of cumulative theory and practice. Unlike the case of the former socialist countries, institutional change in general tends to be cumulative. Much of what we have and do today reflects lingering influences from the past. This is as true of countries undergoing the processes of reform as it is of more stable countries. The result is that the processes of reform are made ever more difficult and complex. Reformers must take into account that old ideas and vested interests never die but withdraw into enclaves, small and large, where their partisans prepare for and await the moment of return. Many interventionist ideas, as we have discussed, promoted more active government involvement and responsibility for the (1) conditions of the economy, (2) level of unemployment, (3) stability of prices, (4) advance of productivity, (5) rate of growth, (6) inequity and injustices in the distribution of revenue, (7) condition of the environment, and (8) quality of life. These are expectations and responsibilities that only a very powerful government and its bureaucracy could meet. Government and its bureaucracy grew and expanded to meet these challenges.[5] Such expansion is certainly more than the liberal state envisioned. This is in contrast to a world of private societies where individuals are free to engage and disengage in trade or any other form of social intercourse and where the supreme social value is liberty.

In its theoretical ideal, market democracy is a minimal state. That is, individual interests are overriding. Happiness, satisfaction, and fulfillment must be sought and can only be obtained by the individual in his or her own way, by reference to his or her own preferences, needs, and potentiality. The social well-being is simply the sum of individual satisfaction, and the social purpose is no more than the sum of individual purposes. Thus, market democracy cast on a liberal state has no purpose and no value other than to facilitate and protect the individual pursuit of personal values and private ends. In this view the state is subordinate to, and intended only to protect the security and property of, the individual. For this purpose it lays down and enforces rules for the exercise of property power, lest the freedom of one transgress upon the freedom of another. It must draw boundaries on the rights of property, lest the claims of one trespass on the prerogatives of another, resulting in endless conflicts between ownership and ownership, between claim and claim. It must provide for the interpretation and enforcement of contracts entered into voluntarily by private parties in the process of exchanges.

Clearly, market democracy as a limited liberal state is primarily juridical.[6] It can do without an extensive and powerful bureaucracy. It cannot, however, do without a strong judiciary. It is a limited bureaucracy consisting primarily of judges, juries, prosecutors, defenders, advocates representing interests before the bar, and police who enforce the rulings of the courts.[7] It is essential to the operation of the market economy. The single skill appropriate to the bureaucrat is that of the lawyer.

By way of illustration, consider the American experience. The American state is basically juridical in character, and until the Great Depression it was also a limited liberal state.[8] By constitutional fiat, as well as in practice, the American state did not have "the authority to intervene, control, plan, direct or in any way significantly affect the cause of internal events, or the structure of relationships, or the distribution of wealth and incomes, or the output of industry, or the character of like, or the nature of the economy."[9] According to this view, bureaucracy as such is singularly constrained in a strict support position to the freely acting, self-interested profit seeker.

The catastrophic collapse of the trading world during the period between the two world wars cast into doubt the viability of an essentially liberal state with its essentially juridical function. The Keynesian Revolution insisted that the economic system is not self-equilibrating and self-adjusting. Keynesians argued that the interwar economic collapse can be attributed to the self-perpetuating insufficiency of aggregate expenditure. Hence, aggregate expenditure must be controlled and held at the level where labor would be fully employed. Only the state, in their view, has the power and responsibility to manage aggregate expenditures.

There is nothing new in the position that the state must bear responsibility for doing what the free market left undone. As we discussed earlier, classical liberalism in the nineteenth century, with its strong bias against state intervention, nonetheless came to perform a host of functions—albeit to service the local needs the market did not satisfy.[10] What is new is that the sovereign power of the state is called upon by the Keynesian Revolution to manage an essential dimension of the entire economic system. The state must now stand responsible for the general level of employment of the country's human and physical resources. The juridical and defense functions of the lawyer and soldier in the limited juridical state are now expanded to include the economist, whose prime task is to manage the country's aggregate spending. This joining of the new professional competence of the economist, the lawyer, and the soldier called forth an expanded state bureaucracy.

By way of contrast, the Marxist perception of the state and its bureaucracy has long remained a critique of capitalism without reference to the deep and both unresolved and resolved problems of every socialist regime. These include (1) the reconciliation of the individual with collective values, (2) the organization of creative change, (3) the recruitment and selection of leadership, (4) the transference and control of power, and (5) the development of effective planning and rationale for collective choice.[11]

To be sure, the classical Marxist conception of the state and its bureaucracy is that it serves to usher in and assure a classless communist society; once achieved, it would wither away. Following the Great Depression and World War II, Western capitalism did not follow Marxist predictions even though organized labor gained and maintained political control of the state and its bureaucracy. Neither private property nor the capitalist mode of production changed as a result of political control by labor. As we have discussed, growing intervention in the economy served to constrain laissez-faire liberalism and the operation of the market economy. The consequent emergence of the welfare state, which curbed capitalism and guaranteed the development of industrial trade unionism, transformed the state of the "dominated" classes. The net result has been to change the Marxist conception of the capitalist state as well.

The neo-Marxist theory of the state now views the capitalist state as functioning with the legitimacy of its authority based on universal suffrage. Thus, it does have the consent of the governed and the cooperation of the dominated, as well as dominating, classes. This is reinforced in part through income transfers and welfare guarantees that serve to satisfy the universal needs of all functional groups. The support is further buttressed through an apparatus of acculturation, socialization, and education that instills ideologies of individualism and nationalism, and through the juridical system that emphasizes values and focuses on private property rights and prerogatives. The net effect is to encourage the development of values stressing individualism rather than collective, group, or class values. The theory thus does not abandon the idea of the state as an instrument of class or the importance of the bureaucracy as its instrument.

Still another perception of bureaucracy is that of the nationalist state. A strict nationalist state typically finds its meaning in war or the threat of war. It develops its strength, organizes all of its resources, directs the energies of its people in a perpetual readiness for, preparation for, or engagement in war. It is a maximal state and usually a military state as well. Its bureaucracy is well positioned to carry out the mandates of a nationalist state; and, as we have discussed, the bureaucracy also promotes nationalism for its purposes.

Thus, the nationalist state puts forth the idea of people who are one and indissoluble, who are bound together instinctively, who recognize their differences from all other people, and who are filled with a national spirit that gives to each a pride, a significance, and a meaning—in effect, one people, one bond, one law, one coin, one sovereign—and a bureaucracy to carry out its interests.

Nationalism represents a collective consumption good or public good whereby its consumption by one individual excludes its consumption by others.[12] The specific benefits of nationalism obviously go to those select nationals who acquire offices or property rights in which nationalism invests. This would include the bureaucracy, the elite, and producer interests. Thanks to the desire on the part of cultural, linguistic, and communication interests to cultivate monopoly power, they are natural beneficiaries of a policy of nationalism, especially of its economic dimension.

If the demand for nationalism as a club good by the elite and the bureaucracy is added to the demand by the general population for nationalism as a public good, it is likely that there will be an overproduction of nationalism. This will tend to allocate too many resources to the creation and preservation of the nation-state, including a formidable bureaucracy and military. It is thus imperative that the bureaucracy and elite be discouraged and, indeed, constrained from the use of nationalism to maximize their returns and advantages.

The growing role of government was not arrested in the post-war period but was accelerated as a consequence of superpower tensions over basic political issues that quickly attained worldwide dimensions. In such an environment, new governments with a liberal orientation did not relinquish complete control of resources for production, research, and development to the civilian sector and the free market. Given the nature of the military and space demands for scientific input, it is unlikely that the civilian sector would have been able to meet these demands in any case.

These circumstances served to reinforce Keynesian ideas of managing aggregate expenditures by encouraging/discouraging private investment through central bank manipulation of money supply and interest rates and judicious budgeting of surplus/deficit at the source of public spending. The justification can be found in the Great Depression, which occurred as a consequence of a downward shift in aggregate spending (producing mass unemployment) because prices did not move freely. Prices neither registered scarcities nor equilibrated available resources to output preferences. Contrary to the neoclassical theory of prices, the evidence suggests (according to the Keynesian view) that prices were administered and controlled in modern industrial economies by large corporations, unions, and other bureaucratic organizations—not a multitude of self-seeking individuals—in competitive interaction-set prices. These organizations have the marketplace in which to set and administer prices. They are not answerable to a wider public, but only to their own constituencies. As a result, prices become a function of autonomous and arbitrary power that is neither answerable for its effects nor responsible for its consequences to society at large.

Efforts to monitor and control the exercise of arbitrary power on the part of these organizations increasingly pushes the government into the formation of prices and wages to ensure desired outcomes. This will typically lead to an increased role for the state bureaucracy to administer wage and price controls. Because wage and price controls inevitably fail, the system is increasingly driven into collective participatory planning where wages and prices are determined—and, as we have discussed, this may, in fact, be desired by some people. Nevertheless, such an arrangement offers little chance that the market system, rather than a bureaucracy, will be allowed to play its effective and efficient role.

The net effects are an ever-increasing role and power for the state's bureaucracy, erosion of the market mechanism, and demoralization of its participants. How can such a growing power be monitored and harnessed, or held accountable, or have its parameters fixed; or how could the electorate participate in the formulations of its policies? One way, of course, is for the state to undertake increasing supervision. However, this merely exacerbates the problem and follows the only too familiar sequence of having the state undertake more control and more complex responsibilities. In this sequence the issue for the individual ceases to be the liberty to choose and decide; rather, it becomes that of accepting whatever is decided upon by the state and the bureaucracy.

Such activity by the state and its bureaucracy is no longer peripheral to and supportive of the operation of the competitive, price-directed market. Indeed, it casts aside the conception at the heart of neoclassical economics of a universe of individual self-seekers in competitive interaction, with resources and preferences optimally equilibrated by a free-moving price, mobilizing and allocating scarce goods and services. In its place comes the view of a world of large organizations, having enormous power to administer and control price as a function of organizational policy, and being neither answerable nor responsible to anyone other than those within the organization itself.

The exercise of autonomous and arbitrary power has also made useless much of the Keynesian prescription that was offered as a cure for capitalism's ills. The supportive manipulation of the money supply, interest rates, and aggregate spending in order to remove unemployment is absorbed by higher wages and higher prices, raised at their own initiative to benefit large organizations. This leaves unsolved the problem of general and specific unemployment. The state is left as the only agency capable of confronting the exercise of such power. As a most likely result, its own power would be increased at the additional expense of individual decision makers.

Perceptive scholars have long called attention to the emergence of a new class, which they have called bureaucratic and managerial. Neither capitalists nor workers were really in control. On the basis of expertise, a new group had insinuated itself into power everywhere. The enormity and complexity of the tasks facing contemporary society have served to promote the interests of this group.

These issues prompt scholars to increasingly devote their talents to determining what must be done to overhaul and direct the state and its bureaucracy to more effectively serve the desires and interests of its electorate. Intelligent and rational constraints must be designed against the exercise of arbitrary power by the state, its bureaucracy, and large autonomous organizations. It is counterproductive to heap abuse, contempt, and new tasks upon these bureaucracies without having a clear idea of what are and ought to be the rules for their behavior.

In another study, I have turned to cooperation theory (as indeed I do in this study) as the theory of public choice, and to economics for helpful insights into bureaucratic and political behavior.[13] According to public choice theory, politicians and bureaucrats are just like other people: they are driven chiefly by egocentricity, not by altruism. For example, the theory teaches that because politicians respond to pressure groups and the desire to be re-elected, the actions of government will often create or magnify market imperfections rather than overcome them. Thus, proponents of the theory tend to argue that the actions of government should be limited. Accordingly, public choice theorists advocate (1) constitutional amendment to require a balanced budget, (2) deregulation, and (3) as recommended in my earlier study, a system of well-defined guides within a lawful policy system of rules to constrain the exercise of preference by the monetary authority for discretionary monetary policy.

Not everyone, of course, is prepared to accept the implications of the economic model for the behavior of the bureaucracy and the political elite. In particular, many are unprepared to accept the constraints on discretionary decision making by the bureaucracy. They argue that impediments such as distinguishing facts from values, the ambiguous nature of goals, and the pressures and costs of information equation cast doubt on constraining the exercise of discretionary authority. In any case, some argue, goals cannot and should not be agreed upon in advance of decisions.

Moreover, critics note that political and economic choices are often conceived of in different terms and are directed toward fulfilling different kinds of objectives; therefore, they should be evaluated by different criteria. For example, Aaron Wildavsky suggests that in a political setting a bureaucracy's need for political support assumes central importance and that political costs and benefits of decisions are crucial. These costs and benefits, however, are very difficult to measure and quantify. Political benefits that might accrue to a bureaucracy may be evident enough, for instance, obtaining short-term policy rewards and gaining enhanced power over future decisions. Political costs might be less obvious and, according to Wildavsky, might need explicit categorization.

On this score he suggests "exchange costs," which are incurred when bureaucracies or political elites need the support of other groups or people.[14] "Hostility costs" may be incurred when, for example, a politician antagonizes some people and may suffer their retaliation. These hostility costs may mount and become "election costs," which in turn may become "policy costs" through the politician's inability to command the necessary formal powers to accomplish desired policy objectives. Wildavsky also suggests "reputation costs," which arise from the loss of esteem and effectiveness with other participants in the political system and the loss of the ability to secure policies other than those under immediate review.[15]

It is also possible, as we have seen, that bureaucracies tend to behave for political reasons, as suggested by Anthony Downs.[16] He describes a group of decision makers as "conservers" whose cautious behavior, minimizing individual or institutional risks, is inherently political. Motives of self-interest, which Downs assigns to "climbers" as well as to "conservers," are themselves political. "Mixed" motives of self-interest and altruism are also partly political. Only the primarily altruistic "statesman" seems to have the general good, not politics, in view. But, as Downs suggests, because the statesman does not compete for organizational resources, his function will simply be underfunded.

Most decisions, however they are measured, have political implications. The choice of criteria by which to measure decisional outcomes has political significance because of the possibility that adherence to a particular set of criteria will ultimately favor the political interests of one group over others. Indeed, caution must be exercised to avoid the unthinking application of economic criteria to the measurement of political phenomena or the assumption that economic rationality is, by definition, superior to political rationality.

Advocates of political rationality defend it on these grounds: (1) One can accept propositions that politics are legitimately concerned with, enabling the decisional processes of government to function adequately; (2) basing decisions on political grounds is as valid as basing them on other grounds; and (3) rationality according to the currency of politics is as defensible as rationality in economic terms. Properly conceived and applied, political rationality can be a useful means for gaining insight into bureaucratic processes.

Traditional conceptions of bureaucracy and its role in government are not altogether accurate. These conceptions are, nevertheless, important in shaping views of bureaucracy. They include political neutrality in carrying out decisions of other government organizations; legislative intent as a principal guiding force for the actions of bureaucracy; legislative oversight of bureaucracy as a legitimate corollary to legislative intent; and direction by the chief executive—which, under separation of powers, creates the possibility of conflict over control of bureaucracy.

In the United States, moreover, significant problems arise form the fragmented nature of the various policy-making processes.[17] The U.S. bureaucracy functions in a political environment where there is no central control over policy; as a result, considerable slack in the system allows the bureaucracy wide discretion. Moreover, not all decision-making power or authority is clearly allocated; this results in many small conflicts over fragments of power. The net result is that bureaucrats in the United States are often active in political roles and take policy initiatives that are not neutral, thereby departing from traditional views about bureaucratic roles and functions. They are, in effect, in a position to develop semi-independence from elected leaders. Their activity, furthermore, is organized around jurisdiction over particular policy areas (e.g., the Federal Reserve Board, monetary policy, and banking). They make a special effort to prevent changes in jurisdiction that might affect their political interests or those of their supporters (e.g., the Federal Reserve Board and its relations with federal and local authorities who deal with monetary and banking affairs).

Bureaucratic power and accountability are major issues in contemporary society. Bureaucratic power is based in good measure on the ability to build, retain, and mobilize political support for a given agency and its programs and to make use of expertise in a particular field (e.g., monetary and banking affairs by the Federal Reserve Board). Bureaucratic accountability, especially in the United States, is difficult to enforce consistently and effectively because of frequently conflicting interests in the legislative and executive branches of government. The issue of accountability is made all the more difficult by the fact that U.S. bureaucracies operate under authority delegated by both the chief executive and the legislative branch, and with considerable discretion to make independent choices (again, consider the Federal Reserve Board and its relations with Congress and the executive branches of government).

NOTES

1. See Milton Friedman and Rose Friedman, *Free to Choose* (New York: Avon Books, 1981) and Milton Friedman and Rose Friedman, *Tyranny of the Status Quo* (Orlando, Fla.: Harcourt, Brace, Jovanovich, 1984). See also George Macesich, *Money and Democracy* (New York: Praeger, 1990) and the studies and evidence cited there.

2. Alexis de Tocqueville, *Democracy in America* (Garden City, N.Y.: Doubleday, 1969).

3. Henry Johnson, "The Ideology of Economic Policy in the New States," in *Chicago Essays on Economic Development*, ed. D. Wall (Chicago: University of Chicago Press, 1972), 23-40.

4. George Macesich, *The International Monetary Economy and the Third World* (New York: Praeger, 1981), chapters 1-2.

5. For a discussion of bureaucracy and its various manifestations, see Francis E. Rourke, *Bureaucracy, Politics, and Public Policy*, 2d ed. (Boston: Little, Brown, 1976); James Q. Wilson, "The Rise of the Bureaucratic State," *The Public Interest* 41 (Fall 1975): 77-103; Anthony Downs, *Inside Bureaucracy* (Boston: Little, Brown, 1967); Harold Seidman, *Politics, Position, and Power: The Dynamics of Federal Organization*, 3d ed. (New York: Oxford University Press, 1980); I. M. Destler, *Presidents, Bureaucrats, and Public Policy* (Princeton, N.J.: Princeton University Press, 1976); Donald P. Warwick, *A Theory of Public Bureaucracy* (Cambridge, Mass.: Harvard University Press, 1975); David B. Walker, *Toward a Functioning Federalism* (Cambridge, Mass.: Winthrop, 1981); James G. Marc and Herbert A. Simon, *Organizations* (New York: Wiley, 1958); Herbert A. Simon, *Administrative Behavior*, 3d ed. (New York: Free Press, 1976); Aaron Wildavsky, *The Politics of the Budgetary Process*, 2d ed. (Boston: Little, Brown, 1974); Samuel Krislov, *Representative Bureaucracy* (Englewood Cliffs, N.J.: Prentice-Hall, 1974); George J. Gordon, *Public Administration in America*, 2d ed. (New York: St. Martin's Press, 1982); Max Weber, *On Charisma and Institution Building—Selected Papers*, ed. with an introduction by S. M. Eisenstadt (Chicago: University of Chicago Press, 1968).

6. Robert A. Solo, *The Positive State* (Cincinnati: South-Western Publishing Co., 1982), 57; and M. M. Clark, *Social Control of Business*, 2d ed. (New York: McGraw-Hill, 1939), 95-96.

7. Solo, *Positive State*, 57.

8. *Ibid.*, 59.

9. *Ibid.*

10. George Macesich, *The Politics of Monetarism: Its Historical and Institutional Development* (Totowa, N.J.: Rowman and Allanheld, 1984), 16-38.

11. Robert A. Solo, "The Neo-Marxist Theory of the State," *Journal of Economic Issues* 12:4 (December 1978): 829-42.

12. George Macesich, *Economic Nationalism and Stability* (New York: Praeger, 1985), especially chapter 2.

13. *Ibid.*

14. Wildavsky, *Politics of the Budgetary Process*, 189-94.

15. *Ibid.*, 192.

16. Downs, *Inside Bureaucracy*, chapter 8.

17. Gordon, *Public Administration*, chapter 1.

8

Centrally Planned Economy:
A "Not-so-nice" Strategy Problem

In essence, a centrally planned economy, or CPE, is typically discussed in terms of its objectives and manner of operation.[1] Usually, it is viewed as the theoretical model of the empirical Soviet model. Indeed, such a view served well for the relatively long period from the 1930's into the 1980's as a number of countries in the post–World War II era patterned their own economies on the centrally planned or Soviet model. It is the model also adopted by Yugoslavia and then abandoned in the 1950's for its own unique market socialism or worker-managed model.

The CPE well illustrates the thesis of this study, underscoring the importance of cooperation theory and of the environment created by various strategies played out in the tournament. In the case of a CPE, a "not-so-nice" strategy was adopted with predictable results.

CHARACTERISTICS

One characteristic of these models is the attempt to achieve rapid industrialization and growth. From posted evidence, such economies appear to outpace market-oriented economies on this score. On such evidence the model was promoted and adopted in the post-war period by a number of countries searching for quick development. It was only with the end of the cold war that evidence became available which indicated the wide gap between theoretical premise and stark reality. Emphasis on such favored sectors as heavy industry, machine tools, and mining—largely at the expense of such sectors as agriculture and consumer goods and services—imparted an unbalanced development that for the most part characterized the economies of countries adopting the CPE model.

Concentrated decision making in the hands of planners operating the CPE model served to promote a powerful bureaucracy with considerable costs to society. For its part, the bureaucracy soon adopted its own preferences (which are not always consistent with the objective of rapid growth) as part of the agenda. The resulting concentration of decision making poorly served the quality and character of the country's development as it did in selecting a "not-so-nice" strategy.

Social ownership of the means of production and the other principal characteristics of CPE well served the bureaucracy whose control over the economy was assured. The CPE thus enabled the bureaucracy to put on the top of the social agenda its own preferences and guaranteed that these preferences would be realized.

For these purposes the bureaucracy put in place an economy with a detailed physical plan and supply apparatus. Such an arrangement is singularly inflexible since it deals with physical instead of monetary or value units (e.g., tons rather than dollars, etc.). It is made necessary by virtue of the fact that prices in a CPE are not equilibrium prices and their use as allocative instruments would not lead to desired results.

This system of material balances along with vertical coordination and control and so-called tacit planning are typically considered as primary mechanisms of control in a CPE. Together with these secondary mechanisms, discontinuous planning, discontinuous incentives, and multiple criteria present the bureaucracy with tools with which to manipulate the economy. Briefly, vertical coordination and control provides the top bureaucratic directors of a CPE with almost exclusive information regarding supplies of factors of production, technology product demand, extent of plan fulfillment and/or lack of such fulfillment from lower levels of the bureaucracy. This also serves to discourage information flowing in horizontal channels and thus undermines communication among operational units, thereby assuring central control by the CPE directorate.

Tacit planning provides the CPE bureaucracy with the means to assure a continuous "sellers' market" so necessary to facilitate rapid growth. The method promotes the mobilization of resources and services to motivate managers of operational units. Optimistic forecasts based on unrealistic output expectations together with unrealistic input requirements of factors of production, and inventory levels lower than required by a given production technique are manifestations of tacit planning.

Given the complications in operating a CPE, it is understandable that its bureaucratic apparatus insists on long-term plans and encourages only infrequent, and indeed discontinuous, changes in the plan. At the same time, the incentive system in the CPE, designed to encourage fulfillment of a specified output pattern, only rewards if the plans are fulfilled 100 percent, while failure is defined as falling short of the established quotas. One result, of course, is that little attention is paid to differences in degree. Moreover, the lower echelons of the bureaucracy are discouraged from "over fulfillment" of a plan for fear that in the future target plan levels will be raised while under-fulfillment will not lead to a lower target.

These issues are further complicated by the use of uncomparable multiple criteria by the CPE bureaucratic directorate to evaluate success or failure of their plans. This is, of course, a consequence of using physical output rather than value of output as a criterion in the CPE. The heavy burden which such a practice imposes on both the information and motivation structures of the economy is a price paid by all for the sake of safeguarding central control by the bureaucratic directorate of the CPE.

PROMOTING A "NOT NICE" STRATEGY AND IMPACT ON ENVIRONMENT

Elsewhere in this study we argue that a "not nice" strategy seriously impacts on the environment in which a strategy operates. By adopting a "not nice" strategy, countries adopting the CPE model destroyed the environment and the very programs and goals their political and bureaucratic directorate wished to implement.

This destruction was facilitated by the creation of a new elite interested in preserving political monopoly and in facilitating rapid growth, centralization, and social ownership of the means of production. The new political and bureaucratic elite and their supporters accepted the new ruling ideology with all the elements, especially the command economy discussed above. In effect, the environment was poisoned by among other factors, political monopoly, administrative inefficiencies, unreliable evaluation criteria, microeconomic inefficiencies, and macroeconomic problems.

The inflexibilities imparted by the highly centralized system have serious consequences for all sectors of the economy. Firms cannot adjust rapidly to changes in production methods or to changing scarcities of various inputs. The supply system in a CPE simply does not provide the correct amount of supplies at the right place and right time. Cumulative shortages occur as a matter of course. Nowhere is the burden more clearly felt than in the foreign trade sector where flexibility is necessary to take advantage of rapidly changing world market conditions.

For all its supposed advantages advanced by supporters of a CPE, it is simply not a system of rational decision making by an omniscient political and bureaucratic directorate. Vested interests within the political and bureaucratic directorate exist and serve as serious barriers to the rational formulation and implementation of plans. Indeed, what typically happens is that bargaining occurs at all levels, reinforcing negative effects of the "not nice" strategy on the environment.

The unreliable evaluation criteria stems in part from the several features of CPEs, such as command economy, priority economy, and closed economy, which immobilize the market price and allocative mechanism. The net effect is to produce irrational prices and arbitrary exchange rates, which lead in turn both to microeconomic and macroeconomic inefficiencies. Again the impact on the environment is negative and counterproductive.

Thus the microeconomic inefficiencies arise from multiple criteria and discontinuous incentives. Multiple criteria may allow lower-level bureaucratic managers to structure plan fulfillment so as to maximize their benefits but not necessarily the intentions of the bureaucratic directorate. Discontinuous incentives lead to periodic supply bottlenecks, poor quality, and a very uncertain production process. Again, the net effect on the environment is negative.

The various microeconomic inefficiencies find their sources in the nature and characteristics of a CPE. Thus the extensive development, pressure economy, closed economy, and command economy of a CPE lead to a slow rate of technological change in both processes and products, poor quality of output, and low productivity of labor and capital while at the same time encouraging excessive inventories of unneeded inputs and unsold outputs to accumulate. The effects are clearly negative on the environment in which the "not nice" strategy operates.

The type of firm cast up by a CPE leads to a pattern of interfirm relationships with a bias toward firms that are too large and not sufficiently specialized. The bias toward large firms and the bias in these firms toward self-sufficiency leads to regional monopolies which, of course, mitigate against optimal allocation at the national level.

The macroeconomic problems of a CPE serve to underscore the other problems we have discussed. Again, the impact on the environment is negative. Thus consumer satisfaction is low in a CPE as a matter of deliberate policy and because of the nature of the model. The reaction to the "pressure economy," the neglect of agriculture under the priority economy, the incentive structure under the command economy, together with an official government policy of full employment lead to a large amount of hidden unemployment of labor and to underemployment of capital equipment and materials.

A CPE, moreover, does not benefit from international specialization thanks to its characteristics, including the closed nature of the economy. A CPE simply does not develop new specialized exports based on present or prospective comparative advantage. Consequently, the country becomes dependent for exports that are currently in excess in the domestic economy.

Various attempts to deal with the shortcomings of a CPE manifest themselves in internal and external safety valves. The internal safety valves include measures to provide flexibility, such as informal decentralization including toleration for outright violation of the system itself. The external safety valves include the use of imports to correct planning errors. Probably the most significant method of adjustment in a CPE is simply to provide for a "second economy" in which, for instance, the social ownership of property is abandoned and private property is accepted.

REFORMING A CPE: AN ATTEMPT TO RESET THE TOURNAMENT

Over time it has become clear to supporters of a CPE that the undesired consequences have become serious. In effect, the "not nice" strategy of a CPE has so polluted the environment that that strategy no longer brought about the desired results. Attempts to reform a CPE can thus be viewed in terms of our cooperation theory to reset the tournament. For all practical purposes a CPE has dug its own grave by the success of its own "not nice" strategy.

Such key elements of the CPE as political monopoly, command economy, social ownership, extensive development, and closed economy ultimately proved its undoing. The prolonged operation of a CPE as in a war economy ultimately erodes the shock-absorbing capacity of its low priority sectors. In terms of our cooperation theory, the pursuit of a "not nice" strategy ultimately undermines the environment so that the exercise of such a strategy is no longer feasible.

Resetting the tournament and implementing a "nice" strategy of decentralized market-oriented economy and, in effect, reforming and/or replacing a CPE is a formidable task indeed. The legacies of a CPE are for the most part negative. Conflicts within the new elite created to serve a CPE cannot be dismissed easily. There are conflicts over objectives and priorities among and between the economic directorate of a CPE and managers, workers, and consumers. CPEs really have no institutional arrangements to achieve organizational unity once ideology and command structure are cast in doubt.

Other key elements of a CPE are also formidable barriers to reform. The interventionist psychology dominant in a CPE and distrust and misunderstanding of how a market economy or "nice" strategy operates leads to half measures, which create more problems, and strengthening opposition to the adoption of a "nice" strategy or reform.

The legacy of vested interests makes reform very difficult. The bureaucracy created by a CPE is after all composed of individuals who now feel threatened by reform. Much the same can be said for workers who feel threatened by the uncertainties of drastic change. Consumers, for their part, fear the price increases of necessities such as housing, food, and public transportation, which typically have received significant subsidies and which reform would reduce.

There is, moreover, little left of entrepreneurship in the environment reduced, if not eliminated, by a CPE's exercise of a "not nice" strategy. These talents are not cultivated in the environment created by a CPE. There is, after all, little place for judgment and personal initiative in a command and priority economy. Rewards in a CPE go to those who can increase output regardless of cost considerations and not to managers who increase productivity so as to cut costs and improve product quality.

It is not surprising that the legacies created by a CPE become formidable obstacles to reform and adoption of the "nice" strategy that reform requires. There exists in the various countries that formerly employed CPE models a variety of pressures and counterpressures which create conflicting or ambivalent attitudes toward reform and resetting the tournament to adopt a "nice" strategy as characterized by a decentralized, private property, market economy. Comprehensive reforms in CPEs have encountered serious obstacles thanks to their very nature and character. These reforms conflict with official ideology, they require significant changes in income distribution, and they disturb vested interests. The net result has been partial reform measures which do not address the interrelated key negative features of CPEs; their failure was predictable from the beginning. Efforts encapsulated to reform CPEs and reset the tournament so as to bring about an environment conducive to "nice" strategy have failed as our cooperation theory suggests.

NOTE

1. For a good discussion, review, and summary of the issues raised

in this chapter, see especially P.J.D. Wiles, *The Political Economy of Communism* (Cambridge, Mass.: Harvard University Press, 1962); Alan A. Brown and Egon Neuberger, "Basic Features of a Centrally Planned Economy," in *International Trade and Central Planning: An Analysis of Economic Interactions*, ed. Alan A. Brown and Egon Neuberger (Berkeley: University of California Press, 1968), 405-14.

9

The Yugoslav Model in Retrospect and the Lack of a "Nice" Strategy

The chief problem in former Yugoslavia was not one of achieving rapid economic growth; rather it was one of efficiently employing labor and capital resources in the growth process and of controlling growth-related inflationary and balance-of-payments pressures. Many more problems, including especially a lack of a "nice" strategy among its constituent republics and autonomous provinces, remained to be resolved as events of the 1990's underscored. Some of these problems arose from of the rapid transformation from a backward agrarian economy to that of a complex industrial one. Others were the inevitable results of past mistakes, including unresolved nationality issues, and of a political monopoly exercised by a one-party system. Although the Yugoslavs were aware of many of these problems, their solution was not always forthcoming.

Before the tragic events of the 1990's overwhelmed Yugoslavia, the country was being rapidly, if haltingly, transformed into an industrial society. It was the first country to try the Soviet centrally planned model and, finding this model unsuitable for its purposes, decide to develop its own model. The period of centralized planning and control, and the subsequent period of decentralization, had convinced many Yugoslavs of the efficiency of the latter way of organizing economic activity. There had been no flight to the market. Instead, the market was being used as the arbiter of economic problems as indeed it must if the worker-managers were to function properly.

The country's early post-World War II experience provides valuable lessons to others that desire to take a shortcut to economic development by the imposition of strong central controls. The principal source of economic progress may well be in the seeming chaos which orthodox planners find so repugnant: human energy, both physical and especially mental, in combination with tools and natural resources, are the producers of material progress. Productivity, however, is the singular problem. Human energy here is the key to the problem and it cannot be harnessed as easily as so many kilowatts of hydroelectric power or tons of steel. It must be permitted free play and experimentation in all endeavors if maximum productivity from tools is to be realized.

The success or failure with which the authorities were able to cope with the country's problems depended on how much scope was permitted market forces in the formation of relative prices (including incomes). The rapid rise in prices prompted the authorities to impose all sorts of price ceilings and controls. However justified by the authorities, controls once imposed have a life of their own. They serve simply to compound the existing distortions in the country's price system. Moreover, they subvert the decisions of the worker-managers, thereby undermining the very foundation of the Yugoslav model. Equally important was a stable and suitable monetary and financial framework capable of serving the unique Yugoslav model. The remainder of this chapter will probe these critical issues as they were reflected in the country's economy.

ECONOMIC SURVEY

This survey attempts to explain the background against which the Yugoslav model was constructed. For this purpose an overview of the country in the 1970's and 1980's is useful. I draw on Dr. Ivo Vinski and his studies of income and wealth.[1]

In terms of the population data summarized in Table 9.1 for the territory of pre-1991 Yugoslavia in the six decades between 1910 and 1971, the country's population increased by about 60 percent. Projections made in 1974 by the Federal Statistical Office and presented by Vinski for the years 1985 and 2000 suggest a doubling of population over the 1910 estimate.

The structural change between the population in agriculture and outside of agriculture suggests that the latter has grown more than five times in the period from 1910 to 1971. Projecting into 1985 and 2000 suggests that better than three-quarters of the total population will be non-agricultural. This shift amounts to a complete change in the relative importance of the agricultural and non-agricultural population between 1910 and 2000.

If we assume that this distribution of population is an indicator of principal source of employment, the change of pace in agricultural employment is particularly distinct between 1953 and 1971 as

Table 9.1

Population—Current Area of Yugoslavia

Year	Total Population in Millions	Agricultural Population in Millions	Percentage	Non-Agricultural Population in Millions	Percentage
1910	12.8	10.2	80	2.6	20
1921	12.5	9.8	78	2.7	22
1931	14.5	11.0	76	3.5	24
1948	15.8	11.1	70	4.7	30
1953	17.0	10.8	63	6.2	37
1961	18.5	9.4	51	9.1	49
1971	20.5	7.8	38	12.7	62
1985	23.2	6.0	26	17.2	74
2000	25.7	4.4	17	21.3	83

Source: Adapted from Ivo Vinski, "Dugoročna kretanja stanovništva i društvenog proizvoda Jugoslavije," *Aktuelni problemi privredni kretanja i ekonomske politike Jugoslavije*, ed. Dragomir Vojnić (Zagreb: Ekonomski Institut and Informator, 1974, p. 112).

compared to the interwar period when agriculture accounted for about three-quarters of those employed. In the two decades between 1910 and 1931 both agricultural and non-agricultural employment increased in absolute terms. The drift in favor of non-agricultural employment, however, is clear. On the basis of these data, up to about 1953 the country is best described as deriving its principal means of employment and livelihood from agriculture. By 1961, however, a pronounced change is visible and the trend continues through the decade so that by 1971 agriculture accounts for about 38 percent of total employment.

Consider now the gross product, summarized in Table 9.2. Vinski's estimates are standardized according to the United Nations concept to make them internationally comparable, and they are adjusted in constant 1970 dollars to reflect actual domestic purchasing power. In the period 1969-1971 seven times more gross product was produced than in the 1909-1911 period. Thus the average annual gross output in the 1909-1911 period amounted to about $3 billion. In the 1969-1971 period the average annual value of gross output amounted to about $21 billion. Projections for 1985 judge these estimates at about $53 billion and by the year 2000 at about $109 billion. By 1985 the estimates suggest seventeen times more output than in the 1909-1911 period and two and a half times more than in the 1969-1971 period. From the results in Table 9.2, we can also suggest the performance of the Yugoslav economy between the two world wars. In the two decades the gross output increased by about 83 percent. In the two decades (1950's and 1960's) following the Second World War, the gross output increased by about 280 percent.

In terms of per capita gross output in 1970 dollars in 1909 and 1911 the value amounts to about $238. By 1940 it was about $320. This is an increase of about 35 percent for the three decades. In the period from 1969 to 1971 per capita gross output was 219 percent greater than for the 1938-1940 period. By 1985 it is estimated that per capita gross output is expected to double and by 2000 to quadruple over the estimate for the 1969-1971 period. Indeed, if the projections for 2000 are in fact realized, then Yugoslavia will have achieved the per capita gross output portion occupied by the United States in 1965.

The significance of these estimates is underscored in the evidence presented in Table 9.3 on long-term annual growth rates for the country. For the ninety-year period from 1909 to 2000, the long-term average annual growth rate amounts to about 4 percent. This compares with long-term growth rates for Western European countries of about 3 percent, for the United States and Canada of about 4 percent, and for Japan of little more than 4 percent.

More relevant, perhaps, are data for the real product per capita

Table 9.2

Gross Output and Population on Current Area of Yugoslavia

Periods	Total in Billion Constant 1970 Dollar	Population in Millions	Per Capita Gross Output Dollars	Per Capita Gross Output Index (1969–1971=100)
Annual Average				
1909–1911	3.2	12.8	238	23
1919–1921	2.8	12.4	224	22
1938–1940	5.2	16.1	320	31
1949–1951	5.5	16.4	339	33
1954–1956	6.9	17.5	391	38
1959–1961	11.0	18.4	596	58
1964–1966	15.8	19.4	813	80
1969–1971	20.8	20.4	1,019	100
Projected				
About Year 1985	52.5	23.2	2,260	222
About Year 2000	109.2	25.7	4,225	415

Source: Adapted from Ivo Vinski, "Dugoročna kretanja stanovništva i društvenog proizvoda Jugoslavije," *Aktuelni problemi privredni kretanja i ekonomske politike Jugoslavije,* ed. Dragomir Vojnić (Zagreb: Ekonomski Institut and Informator, 1974, p. 114).

Table 9.3

Annual Rate of Growth

Period	Total Real Gross Output	Population	Per Capita Real Gross Output
Entire Period (9 decades)			
From 1909-1911 to 2000	4.0	0.8	3.2
Sub-Period (3 decades)			
From 1909-1911 to 1938-1940	1.7	0.8	1.0
From 1938-1940 to 1969-1971	4.6	0.8	3.8
Projected 1970-2000	6.0	0.8	5.2
Non-War Periods			
From 1919-1921 to 1938-1940	3.2	1.4	1.9
From 1949-1951 to 1969-1971	6.8	1.1	5.7
Projected 1970-1985	6.9	0.8	6.0
1985-2000	5.0	0.7	4.3

Source: Adapted from Ivo Vinski, "Dugoročna kretanja stanovništva i društvenog proizvoda Jugoslavije," *Aktuelni problemi privredni kretanja i ekonomske politike Jugoslavije*, ed. Dragomir Vojnić (Zagreb: Ekonomski Institut and Informator, 1974, p. 116).

growth rates. For the same ninety-year period, these rates average at about 3.2 percent for Yugoslavia. Comparison of the two pre-World War II decades (1919–1921 through 1938–1940) and two post-war decades (1949–1951 through 1969–1971) suggest that the rate of growth more than doubled, that is, 3.2 percent to 6.8 percent in the latter decades.

To judge from the evidence presented, Yugoslavia could not be faulted for failing to achieve rapid growth in its total gross product and per capita gross product, two of the more significant measures of economic growth. This is particularly true since the 1949–1951 period, when the Yugoslav model came into force. What, then, of the effectiveness of resource employment? One way to shed light on this issue is to consider the employment of Yugoslavs working abroad and thus in another economic environment. Again I draw on the evidence presented elsewhere by Dr. Ivo Vinski.[2]

Vinski estimates that in 1974 the labor force in Yugoslavia totaled about 9.6 million. The socialist sector accounted for 4.4 million (46%), the private sector, 3.8 million (40%); unemployed outside the agricultural sector, .5 million (5%); for a total of 8.7 million (91%). Employment abroad amounted to .9 million or about 9 percent of the country's total labor force. Germany accounted for about 55 percent; Austria, 18 percent; France, 6 per cent; Sweden, 3 percent; Switzerland, 3 percent; Benelux countries, 1 percent; and other countries 14 percent of the total Yugoslavs employed abroad. The bulk of the employment abroad is located in the West European countries, with Germany and Austria accounting for the largest share.

The evidence presented in Table 9.4 indicates that Yugoslav workers abroad in 1974 produced $5.3 billion of gross output valued in 1970 dollars, or about $5,900 per employed person. By comparison, Yugoslavia's gross output produced by the domestic labor force in 1974 amounted to $26.7 billion or about $3,200 per employed person. This suggests that those employed abroad produced almost twice as much as those employed in Yugoslavia. When working abroad Yugoslavs were simply more productive. Why was this?

Table 9.5 presents evidence available in the census of 1971, which suggests a reason for this difference in productivity. Those employed abroad were more often skilled workers (41%) than is the case in Yugoslavia (26%). Semi-skilled and unskilled workers are almost equally represented both domestically and abroad. The remainder of the skills are distributed in favor of the domestic scene.

One would also suppose that the productivity of those working abroad is enhanced by the economic environment of the advanced industrial states of Western Europe. This is suggested by the evidence summarized in Table 9.6. Accordingly, in 1950 West European

Table 9.4

Gross Output, 1974 in Constant 1970 Dollars

	Gross Output (In Billion Dollars)	Employment (In Millions)	Gross Output Per Employed (In Thousand Dollars)
In Yugoslavia	26.7	8.2	3.2
Yugoslavs temporarily employed abroad	5.3	0.9	5.9

Source: Adapted from Ivo Vinski, "Zapošljavanje u inozemstvu i privredni rast Jugoslavije do 1985," *Aktuelni problemi privredni kretanja i ekonomske politike Jugoslavije,* ed. Dragomir Vojnić (Zagreb: Ekonomski Institut and Informator, 1974, p. 207).

Table 9.5

Yugoslav Employment Situation in 1971

Total Employment	Employment of Those Abroad Prior to Departure	Domestic Employment
TOTAL	100	100
Agriculture	53	42
Non-Agriculture	47	58
TOTAL employed outside agriculture	100	100
Professional and highly skilled	20	40
Skilled	41	26
Semi-Skilled	11	10
Unskilled	28	24

Source: Adapted from Ivo Vinski, "Zapošljavanje u inozemstvu i privredni rast Jugoslavije do 1985," *Aktuelni problemi privredni kretanja i ekonomske politike Jugoslavije*, ed. Dragomir Vojnić (Zagreb: Ekonomski Institut and Informator, 1974, p. 208).

Table 9.6
Per Capita Gross Output in Western Europe

Year	Index (Yugoslavia = 100)
1950	410
1960	342
1970	288
1975	244
1985	207

Source: Adapted from Ivo Vinski, "Zapošljavanje u inozemstvu i privredni rast Jugoslavije do 1985," *Aktuelni problemi privredni kretanja i ekonomske politike Jugoslavije*, ed. Dragomir Vojnić (Zagreb: Ekonomski Institut and Informator, 1974, p. 211).

countries produced more than four times as much per capita as did Yugoslavia. More significant for the country, however, was the fact that this gap was being significantly reduced.

THEORETICAL FRAMEWORK

Too often case studies do not contribute to knowledge because experience is not integrated with research and theory. On this score, the Yugoslav model does indeed have a contribution to make.[3] It is a model based on socially owned means of production, on associated labor, and on worker self-management in production and distribution of the country's goods and services. Moreover, prices, the market, and planning play key roles in the manner and effectiveness with which the worker-managers operate the Yugoslav model in attempting to solve "the economic problem." This "problem" is the multiplicity of ends and the limitation of means with which every society must search for a solution. For their solution to the problem, the Yugoslavs borrowed and adapted theory and experience from early contributors.

Ever since the catastrophic depression of the 1930's, pronounced attempts have been made to mitigate the effects of the operation of basically market-type economies. Such interference in the form of countercyclical monetary and fiscal policies and built-in stabilizers are justified by most economists as assuring relatively high levels of employment and output. These policies and stabilizers have mitigated but not eliminated the business cycle. They have not solved to everyone's satisfaction the problem of economic growth without inflation.

Though the cause of economic planning is advanced in the name of economic growth and development by socialists and some capitalists, the former have at least a greater distrust in what they consider to be the blind forces of the market and in the decisions of people who can only see a small part of the total economic picture.

Even among socialists, however, the role of economic planning in the economy differs. Some argue for rigid central planning, while others temper such planning with relative consumer sovereignty and freedom of occupational choice. In economic literature one of the most sophisticated exponents of the latter approach to socialist planning has been Oskar Lange.[4] The critical issue is that adherence to consumer sovereignty as a guide to production excludes central planning.[5] Advocates of the approach are obliged to show how central planning can be resolved with consumer sovereignty and how consistent pricing is compatible with artificial markets where public managers deal almost exclusively among themselves. The problem of cost calculation and factor allocation in such an economy is indeed of the first magnitude. If in such an economy it is impossible to maintain an adequate pricing process, the guidance of production by consumers is impossible. Central authority will have to rule as in the case of rigid planning by direct decision.

An attempt to solve the pricing problem in such an economy is presented by Oskar Lange. He argues that prices can be determined by the same process of trial and error by which they are determined in the unplanned, competitive market-type economy. According to Lange, the trial and error method is based on the parametric function of prices.[6] To illustrate his point, Lange argues that central planners can start such a process with a given set of prices chosen at random, though in practice the trial and error method would be based on historically given prices. All that is required is that producers and consumers make their decisions based on these prices. As a result, the quantity supplied and demanded of each commodity is determined. In the event that the quantity supplied is not equal to the quantity demanded, the price would have to be changed by the central planners—who would then raise the price if the quantity supplied fell short of the quantity demanded, and conversely. The central planners fix new prices, which serve as a basis for new decisions and which result in a new set of quantities demanded and supplied. Equilibrium prices are finally established through this process of trial and error.

Lange's proposals have been attacked by both advocates of a free-market economy and advocates of rigid central planning. The former argue that such a system of artificial pricing would not obtain desired results because it neglects the profit motive and competition, which are the mainsprings of a market economy. The latter argue against the trial and error method on the grounds that it implies such a degree of decentralization that planned action is rendered almost useless.

In addition to their important role in the pricing process, central planners under Lange's proposal would set the rate of accumulation and in effect determine the division between production of consumer goods and investment goods. Another important task delegated to them is the allocation of investment funds among competing ends. Such allocation would be based, presumably, on parametric interest rates established and continually adjusted by the central planning organization to reflect underlying supply and demand conditions for capital funds.

Detailed production instructions would not be given to the various enterprises by central planners because they lack the detailed knowledge to meet on-the-spot conditions. Contrary to the pretensions of central planners, universal knowledge is not at their fingertips.

Rigid central planners, on the other hand, argue that their central planning organization would be more than simply a price-fixing agency.[7] It is the investment problem and not the problem of consumer preferences that is important. The irrational behavior of an unplanned economy, according to rigid central planners, can be attributed to investment decisions made by many independent units. The centralization of investment decisions makes rigid central planning all but inevitable.

Paul Sweezy, for example, provides us with an illustration of what the central planning organization would attempt to undertake.[8] Once the government has decided on how much of the national income to invest and establishes the objective of such investment, the central planning organization would undertake the drawing up of an investment plan for the execution of these objectives. When the investment plan is completed and the various material and labor requirements estimated, then the consumption schedules are consolidated with the available economic resources to carry out the total economic plan for the period under consideration. Once adopted there are few options left to individual enterprises but to conform with the requirements of the economic plan. The very minor and subservient role played by the price system coupled with the centralization of decision-making powers in a central planning authority stands in marked contrast to the looser planning apparatus espoused by Lange.

Rigid central planning rests on several premises that deserve discussion.[9] First, consumer sovereignty can and should be abolished. Though consumer goods may be distributed through the market, there is no reason for consumers to direct production. Second, the choice among alternative production methods is far less formidable than economists maintain in the literature. Historical, technological, and social factors limit the productive choice to manageable proportions. Third, the longer the planning period, the greater the number of possible investment patterns. These plans cannot be made by independent producing units since they rest on the parallel developments of interdependent industries. Fourth, economic development through long-range planning is far more important than the question of how a perfect static equilibrium can be reached. Fifth, constant checking of the internal consistency of the plan can be accomplished by "balances" so that equilibrium in the development process can be accomplished. Sixth, these balances provide a means whereby the interrelationships of the different industries are known and planned *ex ante* rather than in the *ex post* manner of a market economy. Continual checking of the plan is required as it is carried out.

Implicit in these premises is the assertion that complementarity rather than substitution is dominant in the economy. Such an assertion oversimplifies the problem confronting central planners.[10] As Maurice Dobb writes, "the items which compose consumers' aggregate demand to any large extent form a closely interrelated set, bound together; e.g., by social convention or by links of complementarity between particular wants into 'modes of life' or patterns of behavior which assume the character of organic wholes."[11] There may be some truth, however little, in this view for underdeveloped countries that are too poor for the issue of choice to have significant operational meaning. With development and the satisfaction of so-called basic wants, the issue of consumer choice begins to have some economic meaning. At this stage of development, the consumer presumably is less willing to accept the compromises of his sovereignty required by central planners.

The argument that a more standardized demand resulting from a more equal distribution of income would simplify the planners' problems overlooks the important point that people with relatively similar incomes have widely varying tastes. Moreover, such equality in income distribution tends to conflict with the maintenance of freedom in choosing an occupation.[12] Wage differentials would of necessity exist if labor is to be attracted to various occupations. If these wage differentials are to be more than "window dressing" they must be convertible into claims against society's income.

The second premise of central planning is also subject to question. Unless we are speaking of a world of strict complementarity, changes in production patterns can be brought about even in the very short run. All sorts of changes are possible and do occur. Central planners may choose to act as if they lived in a one-commodity world. Such an assumption would simplify their problem but it would not eliminate reality. Presumably the centrally planned economy would technically resemble the advanced free market economy and, if so, it would be necessary to incorporate in some way the changing circumstances confronting the economy.

The third premise—most often cited in favor of planning— is that it would effectively eliminate uncertainty by substituting *ex ante* coordination in the economic plan for the *ex post* coordination via the marketplace. This of course supposes that central planners possess and at the same time effectively use more information than is available to individual producing units. Unfortunately in bureaucracies, which may be unable or unwilling to act on the basis of such additional information, such planning groups tend to degenerate.

The fourth premise argues in fact that the real test of an economic system as a contributor to human welfare is its ability to develop successfully from one situation to another. According to this view, the planned economy is superior because it is not obsessed with the free-market notion of an optimum allocation of resources among competing ends with both resources and uses taken as given. The reply, of course, is that even a centrally planned economy cannot dispense with the concept of equilibrium. All social economies must attempt to reach positions wherein they make the most of their available resources. Scarce resources must be distributed among competing ends in the most efficient manner if the economy is to avoid bottlenecks and economic breakdown. There is nothing in the nature of economic planning whereby its institution would eliminate the difficult problem involved in the efficient allocation of resources. The concept of economic equilibrium is useful in economic planning.

The fifth and sixth premises and their succession of approximations appear at first glance to resemble the way in which equilibrium is reached in a market economy. The plan grows to perfection, as it were, in a series of trials and errors during which the initial distortions of general policy decisions are eliminated by various experts. The difference between this approach and that in the market-type of economy, however, is that in the centrally planned economy the correction of distortions is concerned only with their removal within the framework of the plan. Such corrections do not overrule the central decision makers.

The most telling criticism against rigid central planning is the wide and embarrassing gap between theory and practice. A prominent Yugoslav economist, Rudolf Bićanić, has put the severity of its shortcomings this way:

> To those who have lived under a system of centralized bureaucratic, normative planning, its expense in human and economic terms and the damage which it can do at all levels of economy are obvious. Sometimes people, particularly economists, are led astray by the bias for rationalization to the superficial assumption that centralizing means greater efficiency and greater speed. The balancing of supply and demand in a centrally planned economy occurs in offices where a few people, unaware of the real effect of their authoritarian plans, become the supreme judges of the destinies of all producers and consumers through their bureaucratic machine. From this source of authority plans lead further down to smaller bodies, splitting unrealistic averages into still smaller averages, according to norms born in offices which, when they reach the enterprise level, have little resemblance to the conditions of actual life.[13]

Professor Bićanić's comments on central planning stand in marked contrast to its theoretical espousal by such of its advocates as Professor Sweezy.

Yugoslav criticism of central planning on the one hand and the free market on the other can be briefly summarized. Central planning, according to their view, leaves very little initiative to the individual to make the best possible use of available resources. Demand and so the structure of production is centrally determined by planners. Enterprises in these circumstances are stimulated to overfulfill the plan by the payment of bonuses and not by additional demand. If the planned demand has been a correct estimate, the stimulation that they received would upset the balance between supply and demand. In addition, preference given to producer goods is raised to a "basic law of economic development" with the inevitable result of underrating consumer demand and thus limiting the freedom of consumer choice.

The free market, on the other hand, is inadequate in their view for accelerated economic development because its low level of demand does not provide sufficient stimulus for the development of key industries. The profit motive in an underdeveloped economy fails to allocate resources in such a way as to automatically create adequate industrial capacity.

The problem confronting the Yugoslavs, as they see it, is how much is consumer sovereignty compatible with planning, which they view as an important ingredient in promoting a rapid rate of economic growth. In effect, they are searching for the proper market-planning mix that will yield the most rapid rate of economic growth and which is at the same time consistent with the country's institutional framework.

According to their view, free-market prices perform two principal functions. They indicate the efficiency of production and they serve as allocators of resources. The first function, they argue, should be maintained and increased. The consumer should be left free to cast his vote according to his preferences for various goods and services, thereby indicating to all concerned his evaluation of the economy's efforts.

On the other hand, allocating resources solely according to prices so determined may not be the most desirous because individual and community interest may diverge. According to the Yugoslav interpretation, this divergency does not mean abandoning the market per se. It means that various methods should be developed for influencing the market so that it will behave in a way that is interpreted to be in the community's interest, especially in regard to achieving a rapid rate of economic growth.[14]

WORKER-MANAGEMENT AND PRICE FORMATION

The country's unique system of worker-management was put into effect with the passage of the "Basic Law in the Management of Enterprises by the Working Collectives," on June 27, 1950, by the People's Assembly of Yugoslavia. The law transferred the operation and management of all factories and in general all economic enterprises in the country to persons employed in such enterprises. The law and its subsequent amendments is based on the principle that though an economic enterprise is public property, it is managed on behalf of the community by the firm's employees.

Worker-management of economic enterprises is thus the foundation of the country's economic system. It is, in effect, the "Yugoslav

Model." Indeed, it is also the principal Yugoslav contribution to Marxist-Leninist ideology. Strict application of such principles of management to an economic enterprise when coupled with the assumption of income-maximizing worker-managers has been shown to be theoretically inferior to existing practices in capitalist firms.

The role played by worker-managers differentiates the Yugoslav socialist firm from its capitalist counterpart in such matters as employment and output. In the short run, at least, the socialist firm departs from optimum conditions of received economic theory. With the same total outlay, the socialist firm employs less labor and more capital than the capitalist firm because when the profit shares of workers are taken into account, the price of the labor input is higher. Its output is also less than that of the capitalist firm.

It is only in the long run when profits are zero that theoretical analysis indicates that both the socialist firm and capitalist firm produce identical outputs and employ the same factor input (labor and capital). Theoretically, at least, such a solution requires free entry of firms into the industry. Unlike the situation in capitalist countries, however, the entry of new socialist firms takes a different path in Yugoslavia. By and large, new firms are organized at the initiative of local heads of government, though private individuals and existing firms play important roles in their inception and organization. This does not mean that the Yugoslav model is unworkable. It means that it is not fully efficient in the usual economic sense.

Important as prices are to the successful operation of the Yugoslav model, much still remains to translate their theoretical role into practice. In the country prices do have a strong administrative component.[15] Shortly after the Reform of 1965, about 70 percent of industrial prices were re-adjusted on the basis of world parity and then temporarily frozen. In June 1966 4 percent were unfrozen, in April 1967 another 1 percent, and by July 1967 another 12 percent. Two years were required to unfreeze 17 percent of industrial prices. By the end of 1967 price formation was formalized by law. Accordingly, prices could be changed by agreement between buyers and sellers provided they were within legal requirements. By the end of 1969 about 66 percent of retail prices were freely formulated.

By 1971, however, the 1967 law on price formulation had lost much of its force and in 1972 a new law effected. Other changes occurred in 1973, promoting various price agreements, but inflationary pressures were overwhelming. Thus between December 1972 and December 1973 industrial prices increased by 17.4 percent, agricultural prices by 21.8 percent, and the cost of living by 20.7 percent. It became clear that government measures to directly control general prices simply did not work when relative prices could not function properly.

This experience led to a move in 1974 to free from direct control seventy-two groups of products from thirteen branches of industry. The bulk of these products had already been removed once before from direct control (in 1972) but placed under control in 1973. By the end of 1974 about 25 percent of industrial products were permitted the influence of free-market forces on their formation. This trend continued in 1975 so that 30 percent of industrial products came under market influence, including such major branches as automobiles, leather, shoes, chemicals, metals, and processed foods. It should be noted, however, that this is not strictly price liberalization as it is a movement toward making use of quasi-administrative measures. It is, moreover, recognized that these measures fall short of the goal of permitting worker-managers freer rein in conducting the country's business. Indeed, it seems that since 1965 whenever the country's announced policy intent is general liberalization of prices and greater use of the market, the opposite in fact occurs.[16]

When we ask why it is that such a state of affairs exists, the answer is that apparently people prefer it that way. Yugoslav experience is consistent with that of other countries. Thus in a 1966 study reported on for Yugoslavia by Marijan Korošić, 62 percent of those employed were favorably disposed toward price control by authorities, 23 percent against such control, and the remainder of no opinion.[17] Moreover, 81 percent of skilled workers are in favor of such controls, whereas only 40 percent of the supervisory personnel are so inclined. Women prefer such controls by 75 percent, whereas men by 59 percent. This evidence is, indeed, suggestive and underscores the problems inherent in successfully operating the Yugoslav model.

Efforts should have been intensified to remove the various restrictions and monopolistic practices that adversely affect the economy. Reasonable "rules of the game" should have been clearly stated and made known to all participants, so that the market and market mechanism would have been allowed to generate the information that worker-managers must have in order to operate the Yugoslav model. This requires, among other things, that prices be permitted to fall as well as rise in response to changes in underlying supply and demand. Yugoslav experience, in consort with other countries, shows asymmetrical flexibility in the upward direction with all the consequences which such asymmetry provides. Various social and self-management agreements regarding prices have not always achieved the desired ends.

It is true that industrial concentration characterized the Yugoslav economy, thereby reducing its internal competitive nature and so distorting the signaling nature of prices. Various market structures such as oligopoly and monopoly were found in the economy. To judge from the scattered evidence available, industrial concentration in some branches of Yugoslav industry was higher than in either the United States or Great Britain, even though such concentration has not always produced the most profitable results in Yugoslavia or in the United States and Great Britain. Concentration in Yugoslavia was even more pronounced than elsewhere in the retail trades. This was made all the more difficult by the existence of small, localized monopolies deriving their strengths from various local government intervention. Appropriate fiscal measures, such as taxes, are needed to extract monopoly elements from incomes derived in such activities, although the appropriate formulas are admittedly difficult to devise.

Some idea of the complications and problems involved in administering prices is suggested by evidence for 1974 when the new agreements on price changes were put in place. Of the 314 agreements which came into force, it took on the average 95 days for permission for change from the authorities. In effect, it took more than three months on the average to obtain permission to make price changes even after agreement on the part of respective buyers and sellers that such changes were in order. Such arrangements hardly make for the price flexibility mandated by the 1974 Constitution requiring decentralization in decision making. It made all the more difficult the resolution of problems stemming from the requirement that losses which had hitherto been covered within an enterprise, thanks in part to price inflexibility, must be directly accounted for by individual units within the enterprise. All this underscores once again the necessity of significantly reducing administrative intervention in price formation in favor of more flexibility and a greater role for the market if in fact the Yugoslav model was to operate effectively and efficiently. It is simply incorrect to argue that the free formation of prices has failed since the Reforms of 1965; the evidence is that such formation was not given a reasonable chance to work.

MONETARY AND FINANCIAL FRAMEWORK

In the Soviet model (or CPE) the monetary and financial structure is relatively simple. Monetary control is essentially microeconomic control. In effect, each firm must work with only one bank, which is usually a branch of the central bank—which settles its debts, in which cash reserves are kept, and which is the exclusive source of credit. It is a very rigid system, one that does not provide for the unplanned generation of finance such as the accumulation of overdue trade credit. In other than Soviet type models, monetary control is macroeconomic. It provides a means for controlling the aggregate level of economic activity. The monetary and financial organization provides the cornerstone for such control.

Providing a stable and suitable monetary and financial framework capable of serving the unique Yugoslav model should have been a top priority item. The Yugoslav model required a means for controlling the aggregate level of economic activity. The country's monetary and financial organization had developed rapidly into a highly complex apparatus, approaching that of the Western market-oriented economies.[18] Efforts toward greater flexibility and use of monetary and financial policy had been made more difficult by growing indebtedness caused in large measure by the failure of "illiquid" firms to settle promptly with suppliers. Thanks to the open nature of the country's economy, the monetary and financial organization could not easily bail out these firms through loosening the strings on credit.

Few countries have elected to copy faithfully any given monetary model. In every case the monetary and financial organization is related to and has grown out of the distinctive economic, legal, political, and social traditions and the objective economic conditions of its specific environment. The Yugoslav case is an excellent illustration. Yugoslavia attempted to imitate the Soviet monetary and financial model—then, disillusioned with that, a mixed Soviet-Western model. What actually resulted is a model that in many respects was uniquely Yugoslav, consonant with other Yugoslav institutions and traditions.

The institutional adjustments in the 1965 reform have had fundamental consequences in the financial field. Further decentralization of economic decisionmaking power, an increase in the role of autonomous economic processes, and particularly the substantial increase in the share of voluntary saving and financial saving formation have resulted in a significant increase in the role of financial variables.

In the monetary field, the institutional changes made monetary processes more complex and effective. The demand and supply functions of money involved new and important behavior variables. As a result, the adjustment processes of demand to the supply of money had become more complicated. Moreover, stabilization goals had become at least as important as production and development goals. This required an efficient monetary equilibrium policy and involves the entire complicated body of problems related to monetary policy formation and monetary policy implementation. Thus, the institutional changes of the reform had brought about a substantial increase in monetary effects. Monetary policy had become one of the strategic economic policy instruments.

The consequences of these changes in the field of financial intermediation were even more important. The changes in saving formation and investment decisionmaking required the comprehensive adjustments of financial institutions, financial instruments, and financial operations, including the organization of efficient financial markets. Under the new conditions brought about by the reform, the financial structure had become responsible for a significant part of saving and financial saving formation on the one hand and economic allocation of the essential part of saving on the other. The efficiency of the financial mechanism had become the essential precondition for the smooth functioning of economic processes and the promotion of a high rate of economic growth. Failure of the financial mechanism would hamper the efficient functioning of the economic system and require a backward re-adjustment of the infra-institutional structure.

Before the 1965 reform the structure of financial institutions involved a central bank, deposit banks, and investment loan funds. It was recognized very early that this structure of financial institutions and their operations had many deficiencies and that plans for the reform would have to include significant institutional adjustments in this area. The principal deficiencies in the financial institutions came from their administrative character and the strong government influence. Investment funds were, in fact, government institutions. Their resources came mainly from taxes, and the allocation of these resources was under tight government control, although effected through granting credits and usually involving competitive bidding.[19]

Banks also were under comprehensive government control. They were established by government bodies. These bodies appointed the management and had a strong influence on bank policy formation. Banks were authorized to operate only within the territory of the government that had established them. There was little room for economic reasoning and free decision making. Such a structure for financial institutions was obviously inappropriate for a system where autonomous economic processes play a strategic role, especially in saving and investment. These shortcomings were reinforced in the new system, where monetary processes and financial intermediation were based on a large body of behavior variables and where financial institutions have to perform a significant degree of economic calculation. This structure was inappropriate even before the reform period, so that plans for its re-adjustment became urgent relatively early. It is for this reason that institutional changes in the financial field were begun even before the reform, partly to make urgent corrections and partly as preparation for the reform. As a result, two groups of institutional adjustments were implemented before the reform of 1965.

First, nearly all investment loan funds were abolished, beginning with the Federal Investment Loan Fund in 1964.[20] Second, new banking legislation was passed in March 1965,[21] introducing fundamental changes in the organization, management, and functions of banks. Both of these groups of changes have significantly adjusted the financial structure to the new needs of financing. It will be seen, however, that institutional adjustment does not necessarily mean functional adjustment. The above measures have only created a suitable institutional basis for a long-run process, that of adjusting the functions of financial institutions to new financing needs.

After a relatively long period of investigation, the banking structure introduced in 1965 and 1966 gave banks far more responsibility for saving formation, stimulation of the supply of financial resources, and economic allocation of saving. Changes introduced by the new legislation included both organizational and conceptual modifications and involved the National Bank of Yugoslavia as a central bank, commercial banks, investment banks, and savings banks.

First, the influence of government on bank policy formation was decreased and the influence of socialist enterprises was increased, in order to make policy formation more sensitive to economic calculation and to the changing needs for financing. Second, in order to improve the degree of fluidity of financial flows, all banks were made interregional and authorized to operate throughout the country. They also were vested with the right to perform foreign transactions with both domestic and foreign residents, provided specific conditions were fulfilled. Third, the new legislation stimulated bigger banks in order to improve the efficiency of bank operations.

The role, organization, and operations of the National Bank of Yugoslavia[22] had not been changed significantly.[23] It remained the central bank of Yugoslavia, performing regular central bank operations, including monetary regulations, issue of banknotes and coins, holding of foreign exchange reserves, and so on. The bank's head office was in Belgrade. In addition, there were six central offices in the capitals of the six former republics. The National Bank of Yugoslavia was an independent federal institution, established by federal law. The role of the federal secretary of finance was reduced to supervision of the legal conformity of bank operations and regulations. The bank was managed by the governor, who was appointed by the Federal Assembly on the recommendation of the Federal Executive Council. He was responsible to both of these institutions for the implementation of bank operations and targets. There was another managing body in the bank: the Council of the Working Community. Its organization and election were similar to those of the Worker's Council in socialist enterprises. Its responsibility, however, was rather limited, and involved labor relations, working conditions, decision making in the field of personal income and investment, fixing fees for bank services, and the establishment of bank bylaws. The council was not responsible for monetary regulations or the performance of other bank operations.

One of the significant questions in interpreting a central bank's position was its relation to the government. As has been stated, the National Bank was an independent institution. It was not, however, independent in monetary policy formation. The Federal Assembly and the Federal Executive Council decided monetary policy targets, and the National Bank played a significant role by preparing proposals and furnishing policy makers with the appropriate analysis for relevant economic developments and forecasts. The National Bank's monetary planning was particularly significant in this connection. Proposals by the National Bank were usually accepted by policy makers without significant corrections. As a consequence the National Bank's influence was considerable in monetary policy formation.

The balance sheet of the National Bank gives a useful indication of its operation. The assets side of this balance sheet is characterized by three peculiarities. First, there are no securities (because of the negligible amount of bonds issued). Second, the main part of the bank's assets consists of discount credits, showing that these credits are the strategic instrument of monetary policy. Third, there is no item relating to a gold (or foreign exchange) cover of bank liabilities. On the liability side there are no specific elements, except the existence of the item related to monetary float.[24]

The banking structure in operation between 1966 and 1990 was hampered by many obstacles. First, the existing structure of investments, which were made during a period when economic calculations played a minor role, proved resistant to attempts to readjust them to the new banking principles. Important external barriers existed that hampered improvement in the efficiency of banking—for example, the still-important influence of governments; an inadequate interest rate policy, which insisted on relatively low interest rates; a demand for financial resources that outpaced the supply because of relatively low risk elasticity, a low interest rate, and requirements for a high rate of economic growth; and a relatively undifferentiated financial structure that overloaded banks. Their net effect was to hamper stronger economic determination of bank behavior, to induce regional confinement of financial flows (under the influence of government bodies), and to weaken bank stimulation of saving and supply of financial resources and economic allocation of these resources. These facts suggest that the main cause of deficiencies in the banking structure came from external sources. This was a significant observation regarding future developments of banking structure, indicating that further improvement of its efficiency depended in the first place on improvement of the external conditions of its functioning rather than on new institutional adjustments. This is also consistent with the old rule that the banking system shares the advancement of efficiency of the whole economy.

In summary, the structure of financial institutions in Yugoslavia was relatively simple. More of its deficiencies can be traced to its functioning than to its institutional pattern. That there were only two of six possible types of financial institutions does not mean very much. There are many economies more developed than Yugoslavia's whose financial structure does not include all types of financial institutions. Deficiencies in Yugoslav financial institutions stemmed from both internal and external causes, though the external tended to dominate. Further development of the structure of financial institutions had been expected to take place. In this connection, the main improvements had been expected from a more realistic interest rate policy, a reduction in government influence on bank policy, more energetic participation of socialist enterprises in bank policy formation, and a surmounting of the historical barrier of the administrative approach to the banking business and the structure of bank investments related to this approach, which had been inherited from the previous periods of rigid central planning.

THE FALL OF THE YUGOSLAV MODEL

In its version of worker self-management, Yugoslavia provided the only real-world case of a socialist market economy. The experience is as instructive as it is tragic. The model appears to have better served the League of Communists, narrow nationalists, and bureaucrats in the country's constituent republics and autonomous provinces than the workers whose name the model bears.

The system of worker management represented a new type of "market socialism" in which workers are supposed to be the key decision makers. In the Yugoslav model social ownership existed *de jure*, but the workers were permitted considerable "ownership rights." No other country attempted to adapt the Yugoslav model, though some tentative steps were taken in this direction by Poland and Hungary.

Certainly, the Yugoslav model of worker self-management did not eliminate the complex problems faced by modern economies. Still, it did provide if only theoretically an attempt to secure more effective democratic control over large government bureaucracies which nevertheless continued to exercise considerable control if not at the federal level then certainly on the republic and local levels in Yugoslavia. Indeed, theoretically, a worker-managed economy ought to require less government intervention than a free-market economy since its short-run employment inelasticity implies that once the system is at a high level of employment and output, it will tend to remain there; the fluctuations intrinsic in a free-market economy will not be present.

The Yugoslav worker-managed firm has been received with skepticism. B. Ward showed, for instance, that in conditions of imperfect competition the labor-managed firm would be more restrictive in its output policy than the free-market firm in equivalent market and technological conditions.[25] The reason for such a conclusion is that the level of output which maximizes average earnings (or surplus per worker) in the worker-managed firm faced with a downward-sloping demand curve is lower than that which maximizes profits in a free-market firm.

At the same time it is also suggested that the worker-managed firm will tend to be smaller than the typical free-market firm in similar circumstances, so that there will be room for more firms in a given industry. Thus a labor-managed economy should be more competitive. Since it would be up to the government to establish more firms as required, a continuing role for government and the bureaucracy is assured. In Yugoslavia this proved disastrous.

As for the theoretical advantage of worker-managed firms and economies to combat inflation owing to the awareness of workers that, all other things being equal, an increase in their remuneration will directly involve a price increase, Yugoslav experience suggests that such a conclusion is overdrawn.[26] In the equally critical area of investment and growth in worker-managed firms and economies serious problems and conflicts arise. Workers may, and indeed usually do, have different attitudes toward investment and growth. There is little to suppose *a priori* that workers are willing to subordinate their own interests to those of society as a whole. And even if this were in fact the case, they may not possess the necessary information to make such a decision.

Potential conflicts between the perspectives of different groups in society emerge as intrinsic to decentralized economic systems of any complexity. They are not dependent on the malevolence of individuals or groups but are rather a symptom of an information problem. There is certainly a need for a central market organization or coordinating agency in the area of investment and saving as Yugoslav experience underscored.[27]

Public goods is another area of government intervention where typically political rather than market decisions dominate. Even in worker-managed economies such goods continue to exist. Again Yugoslav experience in this area left much to be desired. The bureaucracy simply was not able to adequately provide public goods such as health and education, even with comparatively large resources at its disposition.

It has long been the observation of people studying the worker-management model in Yugoslavia that it was not without its specific problems. In particular, there was a need for some central coordination. Such coordination and/or attempts at central coordination of some of the problems common to a complex industrial economy with a high degree of specialization and division of labor collided with the "not-so-nice" strategy exercised by a jealous nationalist republic and ethnic bureaucracy in Yugoslavia's constituent republics and autonomous provinces.

There were and probably still are good reasons for worker self-management as a principle.[28] Unfortunately, the experiment in Yugoslavia was for the most part subverted by the League of Communists, nationalist bureaucrats, and other ethnic extremists—albeit with significant foreign support—working on their own agendas. One consequence of the sad state of affairs in former Yugoslavia is that we have very little empirical evidence of the benefits of worker self-management. The Yugoslav evidence is, however, consistent with implications of our cooperation theory and the consequences of playing a "not-so-nice" strategy and its poisonous influence on the environment.

NOTES

    1. Ivo Vinski, "Dugoročna kretanja stanovništva i društvenog proizvoda Jugoslavije," in *Aktuelni problemi privredni kretanja i ekonomske politike Jugoslavije*, ed. Dragomir Vojnić (Zagreb: Ekonomski Institut and Informator, 1974), 111–17.

    2. Ivo Vinski, "Zapošljavanje u inozemstvu i privredni rast Jugoslavije do 1985," in *Aktuelni problemi privredni kretanja i ekonomske politike Jugoslavije*, ed. Dragomir Vojnić (Zagreb: Ekonomski Institut and Informator, 1974), 201–12.

    3. See, for example, Branko Horvat, *An Essay on Yugoslav Society* (New York: International Arts and Sciences Press, 1969); Rikard Lang and Dragomir Vojnić, "Neki aktuelni problemi razvoja privrednog sistema na temeljima socijalističkog samoupravljanja," in *Aktuelni problemi privredni kretanja i ekonomske politike Jugoslavije* ed. Dragomir Vojnić (Zagreb: Ekonomski Institut and Informator, 1976);

Dimitrije Dimitrijević and George Macesich, *Money and Finance in Contemporary Yugoslavia* (New York: Praeger, 1984); George Macesich, *Yugoslavia: Theory and Practice of Development Planning* (Charlottesville: University Press of Virginia, 1964); *Proceedings and Reports of the Center for Yugoslav-American Studies, Research, and Exchanges*, 21 vols., ed. George Macesich (Tallahassee: Florida State University, 1967-,); Edvard Kardelj, *Pravci: Razvoja Političkog Sistema Socijalističkag Samoupravljanja* (Belgrade: Izdavački Centar "Komunist," 1977); Ljubisav Marković, *Ekonomski Sistem Jugoslavije* (Belgrade: Kosmos, 1977); Najdan Pašić, *The Socio-Political System of Yugoslavia* (Belgrade: Savez Udruženja Pravnika, 1975); Radoslav Ratković, *Osnovi Nauke O Politici* (Belgrade: Institut za Politička Studije, 1977); Berislav Šefer, *Socialni Razvoj u Samoupravnm Društru* (Belgrade: Institut za Političke Studije FPN, 1971).

4.   Oskar Lange, "On the Economic Theory of Socialism," in *Economic Theory of Socialism*, ed. B. E. Lippincott (Minneapolis: University of Minnesota Press, 1948), 55-143.

5.   George Halm, *Economic Systems* (New York: Holt, Rinehart, and Winston, 1960), 166.

6.   Lange, "Economic Theory," 86.

7.   George Halm, *Economic Systems* (New York: Holt, Rinehart, and Winston, 1960), 221 and Paul M. Sweezy, *Socialism* (New York: McGraw-Hill, 1949).

8.   Sweezy, *Socialism*.

9.   For an extended discussion of these premises see Halm, *Economic Systems*, 225 ff.

10.   It also leads to serious theoretical difficulties; George Macesich, 327.

11.   Maurice Dobb, *Soviet Economic Development Since 1917* (New York: International Publishers, 1948), 15.

12.   For a contrary view, see Lange, "Economic Theory," 102.

13.   Rudolf Bićanić, "Economic Growth Under Centralized and Decentralized Planning: Yugoslavia—A Case Study," *Economic Development and Cultural Change* (October 1957): 66; also quoted in Albert Waterston, *Planning in Yugoslavia* (in mimeographed form), 16.

14.   George Macesich, *Yugoslavia: Theory and Practice of Development Planning* (Charlottesville: University of Virginia Press, 1964), chapters 6 and 7 and the literature cited there.

15.   See, for example, Marijan Korošić and Dragomir Vojnić, eds., *Sistem i politika clijene u Jugoslaviji* (Zagreb: Ekonomski Institut, 1976).

16.   *Ibid*., 168.

17.   *Ibid*., 171.

18.   See Dimitrijević and Macesich, *Money and Finance*.

19. These funds were administered by banks, which were obliged to follow the economic plans of the relevant government bodies. In addition to specified projects that had to be financed, the economic plans stipulated for one part of the resources only the purpose for which it should be used, for example, a sugar factory, so that the bank administering the fund had relatively more room for decision making, mainly in deciding which project among many in competitive bidding was the best.

20. Abolishment of investment loan funds does not mean abolishment of a government role in investment financing. Sources of these funds remained under government control, and it continued to play a significant role in investment financing, for example, using repayments and interest on credits as a source of financing.

21. The new banking legislation could not be implemented at once, and a one-year period was granted to banks to adjust to the new legal provisions. These adjustments were not performed until the first quarter of 1966, so that for all practical purposes the banking structure remained unchanged until the reform in July 1965.

22. The bank was established in 1883 as the Privileged National Bank of the Kingdom of Serbia (Privilegovana Narodna Banka) by virtue of the Law of the National Bank. Thereafter the name was changed several times. It was the National Bank of the Kingdom of Serbs, Croats, and Slovenes in 1920, the National Bank of the Kingdom of Yugoslavia in 1929, and the National Bank of the Federal People's Republic of Yugoslavia in 1946. The present name was introduced in the Constitution of the Socialist Federal Republic of Yugoslavia, 1963, Art. 29.

23. The operations of the National Bank of Yugoslavia were significantly adjusted to the new needs in 1961, when crediting of customers was transferred to other banks and the National Bank of Yugoslavia became a regular central bank. Consequently it was not necessary to introduce significant changes in 1965.

24. Monetary float is on the liability side in the "gyro" payment system (European practice). In the checking payment system, monetary float is on the asset side (net), as is the case with the Combined Balance Sheet of the Federal Reserve System of the United States.

25. Benjamin Ward, "The Firm in Illyria: Market Synicalism," *American Economic Review* 48:4 (September 1958): 566-89; George Macesich, *Yugoslavia: Theory and Practice of Development Planning*.

26. Dimitrijević and Macesich, *Money and Finance*.

27. George Macesich, ed. with assistance of Rikard Lang and Dragomir Vojnić, *Essays on the Yugoslav Economic Model* (New York: Praeger, 1989).

28. See, for instance, Jaroslav Vanek, *The Participatory Economy: An Evolutionary Hypothesis and a Strategy for Development* (Ithaca, N.Y.: Cornell University Press, 1971).

10

Encouraging Cooperation via Common Market Arrangements

The brief for and against nationalism has been made on more than one occasion when discussing events in the successor states of East and Central Europe. Many people underscore the dangers of resurgent nationalism. In their view the lid has been taken off the cauldron, and all the ancient nationalistic hatreds are bubbling to the surface. Anyone who wants to preserve a given state as a self-governing entity can also be accused of nationalism and risks being identified as belonging to the forces of evil, in a Manichaean battle between enlightenment and primeval darkness.

Other people argue that nationalism can and does have moral and political value. Indeed, John Stuart Mill argued that representative government was best able to govern when the boundaries of that government coincide in the main with those of nationalities who share a fellow feeling and read and speak the same language. Nationalism has taken many differing forms at various times in different countries. It is probably best to turn to the histories of these countries to explain why any nationalism has the particular qualities it possesses.

Certainly when looking at the history of nationalism in East and Central Europe, we notice that the successor states are burdened by nationalisms that tend to be ethnic. Such nationalisms favor collectivistic and authoritarian political cultures and thus explain the ease with which former communists, with typical belligerence and brutality, transform themselves into ultranationalists. In all cases they are obstacles to the development of market democracy.

Still, it is possible to draw upon our cooperation theory and to adopt a "nice strategy" successfully, even in a hostile environment. For instance, cooperation can be enhanced by increasing the number of participants and more easily meeting a key requirement that participants know they will be dealing with each other again and again. Therefore any attempt to exploit the situation will not pay. For successor states burdened as they are by nationalism of the ethnic variety, participation in a common market arrangement would serve to promote cooperation.

Surely efforts to form regional groups or construct a common market are confronted with the fundamental problems of integrating into a single political and economic entity diverse peoples who are typically differentiated by the distinguishing marks of nationality and nationalism, economic development, and widely varying historical traditions. For insight we turn to the theory of economic integration and monetary policy under various exchange rate requirements.

THE THEORY OF ECONOMIC INTEGRATION

Countries, regions, and communities pursue economic integration for various and often related objectives.[1] Foremost is the belief that integration will increase economic efficiency by emphasizing lower-cost methods of production. By increasing the mobility of factors of production as well as other goods and services, the standard of living is increased. Opportunities for individuals are increased, along with the freedom and range of alternatives available to the individual. The effects of both internal and external economic fluctuations are minimized by integration.

Essentially, efforts to achieve economic integration move one step toward free trade but only within a particular region. The removal of tariffs among members of an integrated unit and their equalization against nonmembers very likely places obstacles, in some cases more formidable than previously existed, against nonmembers. Some experts argue that unless integration occurs among large and economically strong nations, the effect on worldwide economic efficiency is likely to be small. Indeed, these experts assert that integration among small and economically weak nations may actually reduce worldwide economic efficiency because of trade diversion from the rest of the world.[2]

Economic integration can be brought about through a series of steps. The first step requires that participants abolish all tariffs, quotas, and any other quantitative and qualitative restrictions against the movement of goods and services across national boundaries within the area. Such an area is called a free trade area. The second step requires the equalization by participants of all tariffs, quotas, and other quantitative and qualitative restrictions imposed against member countries. This is, in effect, the creation of a customs union and includes the creation of a common agency for the collection and disbursement of revenues among participants according to an agreed upon formula. The third step requires that member nations allow all factors of production as well as goods and services to move freely within the area. No barriers arising from the existence of national boundaries are to be placed in the path of such movement. This is, in effect, the establishment of a common market. The fourth step requires that participants harmonize their national economic and social policies with one another while still maintaining individual sovereignty. This, of course, does not require exact duplication of policies but merely agreement in the same general direction. In effect, this is the formulation of an economic union. Complete economic integration occurs in the fifth and final step. Each of the national entities must delegate irrevocably the control of all social and economic policymaking to a central and perhaps federal type of agency, which then takes over all governmental economic functions.

Since the drive for economic integration appears to be motivated by the desire to increase economic efficiency, it is useful to examine the variables most likely to affect efficiency in a given market area. The greater the complimentarity of the participating economies of a newly integrated market area, the greater, it is argued, will be the gains from union.[3] This is the consequence of increased trade among members. Such increases in trade, however, are typically at the expense of the rest of the world. In effect, the union very likely diverts trade from the rest of the world to the participating countries.

Other arguments reject the complementarity hypothesis and advance the proposition that a union of competitive economies is the more promising, *provided* that large cost differences exist among participants.[4] Under such an arrangement, the lowest cost producers would increase production to supply larger portions of the entire market, while the highest cost producers would shift into the production of goods and services for which they had a comparative cost advantage or go out of business. In effect, a union of cost-competitive economies would create more trade among members of the union. The net result would be an increase in the economic efficiency of member countries as well as that of the rest of the world.

Some economists argue that a union of small countries presents the best possibility because socioeconomic policy can be swiftly and accurately adjusted to changing conditions,[5] the presumption being that a smaller economy responds more quickly to policy changes than a larger. A counterargument is that speed of response to policy changes, rather than the size of participating countries, is the critical assumption since socioeconomic policy changes can be made about as rapidly in large countries as in small. The greater the economic size of the union, moreover, the greater the elasticity of the reciprocal demand and the less the elasticity of the reciprocal demand of the rest of the world.[6] All other things being equal, the greater the economic size of the union, the greater the degree of intra-union trade, and the less the degree of extra-union trade. As a result, the participating countries are better off and, presumably, so are their inhabitants.

Geographic proximity tends to be a positive element in economic integration. Common tastes, habits, and similar cultural and social institutions are all elements arising from the contiguity of national frontiers. On the other hand, such contiguity is often a source of ill feeling, which must be overcome if the full benefits of economic integration are to be realized. Assuming that a transportation system exists, shorter distances usually mean lower transportation costs. Moreover, if the union re-established trade relations broken or reduced because of tariffs and quotas among neighboring countries, a considerable increase in the economic efficiency of the participants would occur.

The height of tariff barriers has had an important effect on economic efficiency. The level of pre-union tariffs among participating countries, the level of tariffs imposed on nonmember countries, the level of current tariffs imposed by nonmember countries on the goods and services of member countries are all factors to be taken into account. For example, the higher the level of pre-union tariffs, the greater are the gains from integration as a consequence of the favorable effects on efficiency resulting from the removal of restrictions. The greater the move by the union in the direction of freer trade, the better it is for participating countries and the rest of the world.

Furthermore, the greater the changes in the location of production, whether within or outside the economic union, the greater are likely to be the benefits from the union. Such shifting is merely a manifestation that enterprises are moving to lower production costs or simply locating new facilities in the right place. In any case, a greater increase in efficiency will probably be the end result.

Even apart from industrial relocation, the movement of labor and capital should make an important contribution to productivity. In general, human capital seems to be complementary to material capital so that educated persons will tend to follow new capital investment. This widening of job opportunities for their graduates should permit institutions of higher education to contribute more strongly to the development of various regions.

PROBLEMS IN INDEPENDENT MONETARY POLICY IN COMMON MARKET COUNTRIES

Economic integration in a common market requires that member nations coordinate their monetary policies to avoid balance of payments difficulties, inflation, or less than maximum employment. Indeed, monetary union is very likely the prime requisite for a true economic union. The coordination of national monetary policies to achieve an overall program of optimum growth for a common market community as a whole is a major problem. Monetary measures instituted by one country have a singular impact on other member countries and may even impede the process of integration or harm the economic growth and stability of member countries.

Nonmember countries can follow quite different monetary policies. For example, one country can pursue a contractive monetary policy to avoid inflation while another pursues an easy monetary policy to combat depression. Within a bona fide common market consisting of an integrated banking system, it becomes difficult to have a monetary policy that differs substantially from area to area. It is likely that the common market would be undermined if the monetary authorities discriminated against one of the integrated countries.

The basic monetary problem in a common market arises from the fact that there are two or more sovereign governments while there can be only one source of money creation in an effective common market. If the government of either Country A or Country B, for example, lowers or raises expenditures, borrowing the difference from its own banks or from the central banks, both countries may suffer inflationary consequences, while only the first government gets what it buys with the money. If one of the countries uses budgetary policy in a conscious and responsible way to combat inflation, it may find itself continually raising taxes and cutting its budget, while the other country, which is causing the inflation by lowering taxes and in general increasing its expenditures, is deriving the benefits. The monetary system and banking system, in effect, constitute a pool of purchasing power available to the governments of the several member countries. An understanding must be reached on how the members will share the available purchasing power.

In essence, such an arrangement must be capable of coordinating monetary and fiscal policy so as to stimulate the centralization of policy characteristic of national economies. At the same time, the operation of such a monetary system must not prevent member countries from achieving what they view as important domestic goals. If it did frustrate such goals, secession from the monetary system and common market would very likely occur by those members who believed themselves to be abused or, at the very least, trade controls of one form or another would be imposed, which is tantamount to secession and disintegration.   Indeed, the balance between these requirements is a very delicate one. It is particularly difficult to achieve in the presence of nationalist aspirations by culturally, linguistically, and economically disparate member states.

MULTIPLE CURRENCIES UNDER A SPECIE STANDARD AND A UNIFIED CURRENCY SYSTEM

A unified currency system or one with multiple currencies provides possible solutions for the monetary problem created by a common market. Interregional transactions within a single country have much in common with international transactions under the specie standard.[8]   In common with national currencies under a specie standard, the currencies of the several regions of a country have a fixed parity with one another. Interregional deficits on current account have much the same effect on bank reserves and the money supply as in the case of international deficits between countries.

There is one significant difference, however. The leverage effect of reserve changes in a region may be less within a single country than between countries. One reason for this is the existence of a regional central bank which may have an adequate supply of government securities to liquidate and thus need not reduce its deposit liabilities to member banks. In addition, the existence of commercial branch banks within a country would enable any branch to run a deficit with the main office as long as the latter is willing to continue to make advances to the branch or take over its earning assets.

Typically capital is assumed to be immobile internationally and mobile between regions of a country.[9] As a consequence, the mobility of capital between regions is assumed to provide an additional equilibrating variable in the process of payments correction. This is in contrast to the standard theory of international trade, which argues that changes in price levels and changes in income are the only equilibrating variables employed in the process of payments correction.

However, there is reason to be wary of the proposition that capital is necessarily more mobile regionally than internationally. During normal periods, capital appears to be as mobile between principal financial centers as it is regionally. Indeed, funds may even move more easily in response to interest rate differentials between countries than between regions. Unlike regional centers where the range of liquid securities may be restricted, the large financial centers with highly developed securities markets may more easily attract funds because of the existence of substantial liquid securities. I have reported elsewhere on the problems experienced in regional centers of the United States, such as Atlanta, Richmond, Kansas City, and Dallas, in attracting funds.[10] In addition, the role of multinational companies in promoting international mobility of capital is often overlooked. They operate in much the same fashion as national companies with regional branches in allocating capital.

It is generally assumed that labor is more mobile between regions of a country than it is internationally. In a country in which labor is mobile, a boom or depression tends to be transmitted over the whole country fairly rapidly. As a consequence, economic conditions within a country tend not to be too divergent. This reduces the necessity for divergent monetary and credit policies within a country.

Labor mobility sets limits to the extent of the persistent divergences of inflationary or deflationary pressures among different regions within a country.[11] This equalizing process is much less effective between countries to the extent that the movement of labor between countries is more restricted than it is between regions of a given country. Of course, the free movement of goods can transmit prosperity from area to area by its tendency to generate an import surplus. If exchange rates were adjusted between two areas for this purpose, the entire process could be expedited. The movement of exchange rates, however, is precluded from our discussion. The currencies of the several regions of a given country are assumed to have a fixed parity with one another as in the case of national currencies under a specie standard. This is tantamount to fixed exchange rates.

FLEXIBLE EXCHANGE RATES

Another possible solution to the monetary problem is to tie the common market together at the economic level with flexible exchange rates. Such an arrangement is especially suitable when a common market is to consist of culturally, linguistically, and economically disparate members. It would permit each member to develop its economy within the confines of its territory according to its own appraisal of possibilities. Flexible exchange rates provide an "automatic" trade balancing mechanism, thereby eliminating the necessity for exchange and trade controls.[12] At the same time, the individual nations are freed from having to coordinate monetary and fiscal policies and economic development programs with other nations.

Encroachment into the delicate area of nationalist sovereignty is minimized. As a consequence, the chances for a successful common market are improved.

A system of flexible exchange rates would also help compensate for the "stickiness" of wages and prices brought about by different stages of economic development among the member states of a common market. By promoting what would partially deputize for competitive price flexibility, flexible exchange rates would increase the effectiveness of the price mechanism and thus contribute to legitimate economic integration. Such an arrangement provides a means for combining interdependence among member countries through trade with the greatest possible amount of internal monetary and fiscal independence. No member country would be able to impose its policy mistakes on others nor would it have their mistakes imposed on itself. Each country would be free to pursue policies for internal stability according to its own appraisal of possibilities. If all member countries succeeded in their internal policies, reasonably stable exchange rates would prevail. Effective intercountry coordination would be achieved without the risks of formal but ineffective coordination.

On the other hand, critics of a system of flexible exchange rates argue that an exchange rate left to find its own level will not necessarily trace out an optimum path through time. However, an optimum is very difficult to define since its criteria hinge on medium-term and long-term expectations which can never be guaranteed.[13] Nevertheless, there is no necessity that the market per se will yield a reasonably satisfactory rate. Moreover, in small undiversified and less-developed countries, which may be members of the common market, a lack of sophisticated individuals with a heterogenous outlook and sufficient capital may impair the working of a competitive market in foreign exchange.

Another criticism is that exchange rate adjustments will not necessarily insulate the level of domestic activity while correcting an internal balance.[14] Exchange rate adjustments are particularly desirable when price levels have moved out of line. The exchange rate correction will restore the terms of trade to their original position and leave the volume and balance of trade and real income in each country at their original levels. The units of measurement will simply be changed. This is no longer true where the sources of disturbance are structural changes in trading regions, different rates of full employment growth in several regions joined in a common market, and cyclical income fluctuations. Repercussions on domestic employment and output can be reduced, but they apparently cannot be eliminated by flexible exchange rates.

The case for flexible exchange rates, however, appears to gather strength in a multinational common market where labor immobility caused by cultural differences exists or where a central government does not exist; if it does exist, it is indifferent or incapable of assuming responsibility for easing a depressed or less-developed region's adjustments. It may be just such a case that recent writers have in mind when they argue that if a common market is divided into national regions, there is within each a factor mobility and between which there is a factor immobility, then each region can have a separate currency which fluctuates relative to all other currencies.[15] In this case, the national region as an economic unit and currency domain coincide. Moreover, the stabilization argument for flexible exchange rates is valid when based on regional currency areas.

NOTES

1.   See Bela Belassa, *The Theory of Economic Integration* (Homewood, Ill.: Richard D. Irwin, 1961); James E. Meade, *Problem of Economic Union* (Chicago: University of Chicago Press, 1953); Paul Streeten, *Economic Integration: Aspects and Problems* (Leyden: A. W. Sythoff, 1961); Jacob Viner, *The Customs Unions Issue* (New York: Carnegie Endowment for International Peace, 1950); Harry G. Johnson, *Money, Trade and Economic Development* (London: George Allen and Unwin, 1962); Tibor Scitovsky, *Economic Theory and Western European Integration* (Stanford, Calif.: Stanford University Press, 1958).

2.   Cf. Viner, *Customs Union*, 135ff.

3.   Cf. Belassa, *Economic Integration*, 26-61.

4.   Cf. Viner, *Customs Union*, 51.

5.   Cf. Belassa, *Economic Integration*.

6.   Cf. Viner, *Customs Union*.

7. See M. R. Colberg, "The Theory of Human Capital Movement," in *Human Capital in Southern Development, 1939-1963* (Chapel Hill: University of North Carolina Press, 1963).

8.   Franz Gehrels, "Monetary Systems for the Common Market," *Journal of Finance* (May 1959): 312-21; and George Macesich, *Commercial Banking and Regional Development in the United States, 1950-60* (Tallahassee: Florida State University Press, 1965).

9. J. C. Ingram argues that regions can borrow or sell securities in the national capital market more easily than countries can borrow abroad. See his contribution in *Factors Affecting the United States Balance of Payments* (Washington: U.S. Government Printing Office, 1962). For a lucid discussion of these issues, see Peter P. Kenen,

"Toward a Supranational Monetary System" in *Issues in Banking and Monetary Analysis* ed. G. Pontecorvo, R. P. Shay and A. G. Hart (New York: Holt, Rinehart, and Winston, 1967).

10. See reference in footnote 8. My own observations would agree in part with those of Franz Gehrels, "Monetary Systems," 313, when he writes: "National financial centers are well-developed markets with plenty of highly liquid securities; regional centers are much less able to attract funds. What they do instead is to liquidate government securities or widely accepted private obligations in the national center. An inflow of funds from Paris to Frankfurt might normally be easier to bring about than one from San Francisco to Kansas City." Wilson E. Schmidt writes that before the Interest Equalization Tax, a substantial portion—some guesses as high as 50 percent of foreign dollar public issues sold in New York—was bought by foreigners. This was a way for foreigners to avoid their own inefficient markets and shift funds from low to high yields within their own areas. See his "Commentary" in I. O. Scott's paper in Pontecorvo, *et al.*, *Banking and Monetary Analysis*, 203-5.

11. See Robert A. Mundell, "A Theory of Optimum Currency Areas," *American Economic Review* (September 1961): 657-64; and Ronald I. McKinnon, "Optimum Currency Areas," *American Economic Review* (September 1963): 717-25. Kenen, on the other hand, argues that a diversification of output and internal labor mobility, geographic, and occupational may serve as effective substitutes for the international or interregional labor mobility emphasized by recent writers. Such diversification of output, moreover, may serve to avoid painful adjustments because of insufficient averaging of trade-balance disturbances. In such cases, large changes in trade may be needed to re-establish external and internal balance. "Supranational Monetary System," 218-20.

12. See L. B. Yeager, "Exchange Rates Within a Common Market," *Social Research* (January 1959): 415-38. My own published material relevant to the topic includes: George Macesich, *Yugoslavia: Theory and Practice of Development Planning* (Charlottesville: University Press of Virginia, 1964); "The Theory of Economic Integration and the Experience of the Balkan and Danubian Countries Before 1914" (A paper delivered before the 1st International Congress on Southeastern European Studies, Sofia, Bulgaria, August-September, 1966), *The Florida State University Slavic Papers*, vol. 1 (1967); "Economic Theory and the Austro Hungarian Ausgleich" (A paper prepared for the International Congress on the Austro-Hungarian Ausgleich of 1867, Bratislava, Czechoslovakia, August 28 - September 2, 1967, *Proceedings of the Congress*; "Inflation and the Common Market," *Review of International Affairs* (5 June 1964); "Supply and Demand

for Money in Canada," in *Varieties of Monetary Experience* ed. Milton Friedman and David Meiselman (Chicago: University of Chicago Press, 1969); *Money in a European Common Market Setting* (Baden-Baden: Nomos Veriagsgesellschaft, 1972); *Economic Nationalism and Stability* (New York: Praeger, 1985).

13. See George Halm, "The Case for Greater Exchange-Rate Flexibility in an Interdependent World," and Albert G. Hart, "Commentary," in Pontecarvo, *et al.*, eds., *Banking and Monetary Analysis*: 169-88.

14. See Gehrels, "Monetary Systems," 319.

15. See Mundell, "Optimum Currency Rates," 663-64. See also, "Europe's Monetary Future," *The Economist*, 23 October 1993, pp. 25-27.

Bibliography

Allen, W. R. "Irving Fisher, FDR, and the Great Depression." *History of Political Economy* (Winter 1977): 560-87.

Alpert, Paul. *Twentieth Century Economic History of Europe*. New York: Henry Schuman, 1951.

Arndt, H. W. *The Economic Lessons of the Nineteen Thirties*. London: Frank Cass and Co., 1963.

Axelrod, Robert. *Evolution of Cooperation*. New York: Basic Books, 1984.

Axelrod, Robert, and William D. Hamilton. "The Evolution of Cooperation." *Science* 27 March 1981, 1390-96.

Bagehot, Walter. *Lombard Street*. Reprint. New York: Arno Press, 1969.

Belassa, Bela. *The Theory of Economic Integration*. Homewood, Ill.: Richard D. Irwin, 1961.

Belassa, B., and R. Nelson, eds. *Economic Progress, Private Values, and Public Policy: Essays in Honor of William Felnew*. Amsterdam: North-Holland Publishing Co., 1977.

Bićanić, Rudolf. "Economic Growth Under Centralized and Decentralized Planning: Yugoslavia—A Case Study." *Economic Development and Cultural Change* (October 1957): 66-70.

Bloomfield, Arthur I. *Monetary Policy Under the International Gold Standard: 1880-1914*. New York: Federal Reserve Bank of New York, 1959.

Bonn, Moritz J. *The Crumbling of Empire: The Disintegration of World Economy*. London: George Allen and Unwin, 1938.

Brown, Alan A., and Egon Neuberger. "Basic Features of a Centrally Planned Economy," in *International Trade and Central Planning:*

An Analysis of Economic Interactions, edited by Alan A. Brown and Egon Neuberger, 405-14. Berkeley: University of California Press, 1968.

Buchanan, James M. "Politics, Policy and the Pigovian Margins." *Economics* (February 1962): 17-24.

Buchanan, James. "Socialism Is Dead: Leviathan Lives." *Wall Street Journal* 18 July 1990, p. A10.

Cagan, Phillip. "The Monetary Dynamics of Hyperinflation," in *Studies in the Quantity Theory of Money*, edited by Milton Friedman, 25-117. Chicago: University of Chicago Press, 1956.

Cantillon, Richard. *Essai sur la nature du commerce en général-1734*. Translated and edited by Henry Higgs, London. Reissued for Royal Economic Society by Frank Cass and Co., 1959.

Claghan, John H. "Europe After the Great Wars, 1816 and 1920." *Economic Journal* (December 1920): 423-35.

Clark, M. M. *Social Control of Business*. 2d ed. New York: McGraw-Hill, 1939.

Coase, Ronald H. "The Problem of Social Cost." *Journal of Law and Economics* (October 1960): 1-44.

Cohen, M., T. Nagel, and T. Scanlon, eds. *War and Moral Responsibility*. Princeton, N.J.: Princeton University Press, 1974.

Colberg, M. R. "The Theory of Human Capital Movement." In *Human Capital in Southern Development, 1939-1963*, 30-54. Chapel Hill: University of North Carolina Press, 1963.

Commons, John R. *The Economics of Collective Action*. New York: Macmillan, 1950.

Day, John P. *Introduction to World Economic History Since the Great War*. London: Macmillan & Company, Ltd., 1939.

de Tocqueville, Alexis. *Democracy in America*. Garden City, N.Y.: Doubleday, 1969.

Destler, I. M. *Presidents, Bureaucrats, and Public Policy*. Princeton, N.J.: Princeton University Press, 1976.

Dimitrijević, Dimitrije, and George Macesich. *Money and Finance in Contemporary Yugoslavia: A Comparative Analysis*. New York: Praeger, 1984.

Dimitrijević, Dimitrije, and George Macesich. *The Money Supply Process: A Comparative Analysis*. New York: Praeger, 1991.

Dobb, Maurice. *Soviet Economic Development Since 1917*. New York: International Publishers, 1948.

Dorfman, J. *The Economic Mind in American Civilization*. New York: Viking Press, 1949.

Downs, Anthony. *Inside Bureaucracy*. Boston: Little, Brown, 1967.

Eckstein, Alexander, ed. *Comparisons of Economic Systems: Theoretical and Methodological Approaches*. Berkeley: University of California Press, 1971.

"Exchange Rates." Editorial. *The Economist* 25 July 1992, pp. 15-16.

Frenkel, Jacob A. "Adjustment Lags versus Information Lags: A 'Comment' and 'Reply' by Charles R. Nelson." *Journal of Money, Credit, and Banking* (November 1981): 490-96.

Frenkel, Jacob A., and Harry G. Johnson, ed. *The Monetary Approach to the Balance of Payments*, chapter 16. Toronto: University of Toronto Press, 1976.

Friedman, Milton. "Déjà Vu in Currency Markets." *Wall Street Journal* 22 September 1992, p. A18.

Friedman, Milton. "A Monetarist Reflects." *The Economist* 4 June 1983, pp. 17-19.

Friedman, Milton, and Rose Friedman. *Free to Choose*. New York: Avon Books, 1981.

Friedman, Milton, and Rose Friedman. *Tyranny of the Status Quo.* Orlando, Fla.: Harcourt, Brace, Jovanovich, 1984.

Friedman, Milton, and Anna J. Schwartz. *A Monetary History of the U.S., 1867-1960.* Princeton, N.J.: Princeton University Press, 1963.

Friedman, Milton, and Anna J. Schwartz. *Monetary Trends in the United States and United Kingdom: Their Relation to Revenue, Price, and Interest Rates, 1867-1975.* Chicago: University of Chicago Press, 1982.

Fukuyama, Francis. "Rest Easy, It's Not 1914 Anymore." *New York Times* 9 February 1992.

Galbraith, John Kenneth. "Came the Revolution." Review of Keynes' *General Theory*. *New York Times Book Review* 16 May 16, 1965.

Galbraith, J. K. *The Great Crash*. Boston: Houghton Mifflin, 1972.

Gehrels, Franz. "Monetary Systems for the Common Market." *Journal of Finance* (May 1959): 312-21.

Gordon, George J. *Public Administration in America*. 2d ed. New York: St. Martin's Press, 1982.

Gregory, P. R., and R. C. Stuart. *Comparative Economic Systems*. 3d ed. Boston: Houghton Mifflin Co., 1985.

Gregory, Theodore E. "The Economic Significance of 'Gold Maldistribution.'" *Manchester School of Economics and Social Studies*, vol. 2, no. 2 (1931):77.

Gregory, Theodore E. *Gold, Unemployment and Capitalism*. London: P. S. King and Son, 1933.

Gregory, Theodore E. *The Gold Standard and Its Future*. 3d ed. New York: E. P. Dutton and Co., 1935.

Gregory, Theodore E. "Rationalization and Technological Unemployment." *Economic Journal* (December 1930): 441-67.

Guillebaud, Claude W. *The Economic Recovery of Germany, from*

1933 to the Incorporation of Austria in March, 1938. London: Macmillan and Co., 1939.

Habler, Gottfried. Review of the Johnson and Frenkel compilation of studies. *Journal of Economic Literature* (December 1976): 1324-28.

Halm, George. "The Case for Greater Exchange-Rate Flexibility in an Interdependent World," in *Issues in Banking and Monetary Analysis*, edited by G. Pontecorvo, R. P. Shay and A. G. Hart. New York: Holt, Rinehart, and Winston, 1967.

Halm, George. *Economic Systems.* New York: Holt, Rinehart, and Winston, 1960.

Hamilton, E. J., A. Rees, and H. G. Johnson, eds. *Landmarks in Political Economy.* Selections from the Journal of Political Economy. Chicago: University of Chicago, 1962.

Hart, Albert G. "Commentary," in G. Pontecorvo, R. P. Shay and A. G. Hart. *Issues in Banking and Monetary Analysis*, 169-88. New York: Holt, Rinehart, and Winston, 1967.

Hayek, F. A. "The Austrian Critique." *The Economist* 11 June 1983, pp. 39-41.

Hayek, F. A. *Studies in Philosophy, Politics, and Economics.* Chicago: University of Chicago Press, 1967.

Herren, Robert. "Review of Moggridge's *Collected Writings of John Maynard Keynes.*" *Journal of Economic History* (June 1980): 451-52.

Hicks, John. "A Skeptical Follower." *The Economist* 18 June 1983, pp. 17-19.

Hobson, John. *Imperialism.* London: George Allen and Unwin, 1902.

Hofstadter, Douglas R. "Metamagical Themas." *Scientific American* (May 1983): 16-26.

Hoover, Calvin B. *Memories of Capitalism, Communism, and Nazism.* Durham, N.C.: Duke University Press, 1965.

Horvat, Branko. *An Essay on Yugoslav Society.* New York: International Arts and Sciences Press, 1969.

Hume, David. "Of Interest; Of Money." in *Essays, Moral, Political, and Literary*, vol. 1 of *Essays and Treatises.* Edinburgh: Bell and Bradfute, Cadell, and Davis, 1804.

Hunt, E. K. *History of Economic Thought: A Critical Perspective.* Belmont, Calif.: Wadsworth, 1979.

Hutchinson, Keith. *The Decline and Fall of British Capitalism.* New York: Charles Scribner's Sons, 1950.

Ingram, J. C. *Factors Affecting the United States Balance of Payments.* Washington: U.S. Government Printing Office, 1962.

Johnson, E., ed. *The Collected Writings of John Maynard Keynes, Activities 1920-1922*, vol. 17, *Treaty Revision and Reconstruction*,

Vol. 18, *Activities: 1922-1932: The End of Reparations.* London: Macmillan; New York: Cambridge University Press for the Royal Economic Society.

Johnson, Harry G. *Money, Trade and Economic Development.* London: George Allen and Unwin, 1962.

Johnson, Henry. "The Ideology of Economic Policy in the New States," in *Chicago Essays on Economic Development*, edited by D. Wall, 23-40. Chicago: University of Chicago Press, 1972.

Kahn, Alfred E. *Great Britain in the World Economy.* New York: Columbia University Press, 1946.

Kardelj, Edvard. *Pravci: Razvoja Političkog Sistema Socijalističkag Samoupravljanja.* Beograd: Izdavački Centar "Komunist," 1977.

Kenen, Peter P. "Toward a Supranational Monetary System" in *Issues in Banking and Monetary Analysis*, edited by G. Pontecorvo, R. P. Shay and A. G. Hart, pp. 77-80. New York: Holt, Rinehart, and Winston, 1967.

Keynes, John M. "The City of London and the Bank of England, August 1914." *Quarterly Journal of Economics* (November 1914): 48-71.

Keynes, John M. *The Economic Consequences of Mr. Churchill.* London: Leonard and Virginia Woolf, 1925.

Keynes, John M. *The Economic Consequences of the Peace.* London: Macmillan and Co., 1920.

Keynes, John M. "The Economics of War in Germany." *Economic Journal* (September 1914): 442-52

Keynes, John M. *The End of Laissez-Faire.* London: Leonard and Virginia Woolf, 1927.

Keynes, John M. *Essays in Persuasion.* New York: Harcourt, Brace and Co., 1932.

Keynes, John M. "The French Stabilization Law." *Economic Journal* (September 1928): 490-94.

Keynes, John Maynard. *General Theory of Employment, Interest, and Money.* New York: Harcourt, Brace, and Co., 1936

Keynes, John M. "The German Transfer Problem." *Economic Journal* (March 1929): 107.

Keynes, John M. *A Revision of the Treaty.* London: Macmillan and Co., 1922.

Keynes, John M. "A Short View of Russia," in *Essays in Persuasion.* New York: Harcourt, Brace, 1932.

Keynes, John M. *Treatise on Money.* London: MacMillan, 1930; New York: St. Martin's Press, 1971.

Keynes, John M. "War and the Financial System, August 1914." *Economic Journal* (September 1914): 460-86.

Keynes, John M. with H. D. Henderson. *Can Lloyd George Do It? An*

Examination of the Liberal Pledge. London: Nation and Athenaeum, 1919.

Keynes, Milo, ed. *Essays on John Maynard Keynes.* New York and London: Cambridge University Press, 1975.

Kindleberger, Charles P. *Economic Development.* New York: McGraw-Hill, 1958.

Knight, Frank H. *The Ethics of Competition.* New York: Augustus M. Kelley, 1950.

Koopmans, T. C., and J. M. Montias. "On the Description and Comparisons of Economic Systems," in *Comparison of Economic Systems: Theoretical and Methodological Approaches,* edited by Alexander Eckstein, 29-78. Berkeley: University of California Press, 1971.

Korošić, Marijan, and Dragomir Vojnić, eds. *Sistem i politika cli jene u Jugoslaviji.* Zagreb: Ekonomski Institut, 1976.

Krislov, Samuel. *Representative Bureaucracy.* Englewood Cliffs, N.J.: Prentice-Hall, 1974.

Lang, Rikard, and Dragomir Vojnić. "Neki aktuelni problemi razvoja privrednog sistema na temeljima socijalističkog samoupravljanja," in *Aktuelni problemi privredni kretanja i ekonomske politike Jugoslavije,* edited by Dragomir Vojnić. Zagreb: Ekonomski Institut and Informator, 1976.

Lange, Oskar. "On the Economic Theory of Socialism," in *Economic Theory of Socialism,* edited by B. E. Lippincott, 55-143. Minneapolis: University of Minnesota Press, 1948.

Lange, Oskar, and Fred M. Taylor. *On the Economic Theory of Socialism,* edited by Benjamin E. Lippincott. Minneapolis: University of Minnesota Press, 1938.

Law, John. *Money and Trade consider'd with a Proposal for Supplying the Nation with Money.* 2d ed. Edinburgh: Anderson, 1720.

League of Nations. *The Network of World Trade.* Geneva: League of Nations, 1932-1944.

League of Nations. *World Economic Survey.* Geneva: League of Nations, 1932-1944.

Lerner, Abba P. "Statics and Dynamics in Socialist Economies." *Economic Journal* vol. 47, no. 186 (June 1937): 263-67.

Lindbeck, Asser. *The Political Economy of the New Left: An Outsider's View.* 2d ed. New York: Harper and Row, 1977.

Lodge, George C. *The New American Ideology.* New York: Alfred A. Knopf, 1975.

Luce, D. and H. Raiffa. *Games and Decisions.* New York: John Wiley and Sons, 1975.

Macesich, George. *Commercial Banking and Regional Development in the United States, 1950-60.* Tallahassee: Florida State University Press, 1965.

Macesich, George. "Current Inflation Theory: Consideration of Methodology." *Social Research* (Autumn 1961): 321-30.

Macesich, George. *Economic Nationalism and Stability.* New York: Praeger, 1985.

Macesich, George. "Economic Theory and the Austro Hungarian Ausgleich." A paper prepared for the International Congress on the Austro-Hungarian Ausgleich of 1867, Bratislava, Czechoslovakia, August 28-September 2, 1967. *Proceedings of the Congress.*

Macesich, George. "Inflation and the Common Market." *Review of International Affairs* 5 June 1964.

Macesich, George. *The International Monetary Economy and the Third World.* New York: Praeger, 1981.

Macesich, George. "International Trade and United States Economic Development Revisited." *Journal of Economic History,* September 1961, reprinted in Stanley Cohen and Forest Hill, eds. *American Economic History: Essay in Interpretation.* Philadelphia: J. B. Lippincott, 1966.

Macesich, George. "Monetary Policy and International Interdependence in the Great Depression: The U.S. and Yugoslavia." *Zbornik.* Belgrade: Serbian Academy of Sciences and Arts, 1976.

Macesich, George. *Monetary Reform and Cooperation Theory.* New York: Praeger, 1989.

Macesich, George. *Money and Democracy.* New York: Praeger, 1990.

Macesich, George. *Money in a European Common Market Setting.* Baden-Baden: Nomos Veriagsgesellschaft, 1972.

Macesich, George. *The Politics of Monetarism: Its Historical and Institutional Development.* Totowa, N.J.: Rowman and Allanheld, 1984.

Macesich, George. *Proceedings and Reports of the Center for Yugoslav-American Studies, Research, and Exchanges,* 21 vols., edited by George Macesich. Tallahassee, Fla.: Florida State University, 1967-.

Macesich, George. "The Quantity Theory and the Revenue Expenditure Theory in an Open Economy: Canada 1926-58." *The Canadian Journal of Economics and Political Science* (August 1964): 368-90.

Macesich, George. *Reform and Market Democracy.* New York: Praeger, 1991.

Macesich, George. "The Sources of Monetary Disturbances in the United States, 1834-45." *Journal of Economic History* (September 1960): 407-34.

Macesich, George. "Supply and Demand for Money in Canada," in *Varieties of Monetary Experience*, edited by Milton Friedman and David Meiselman, 249-91. Chicago: University of Chicago Press, 1969.

Macesich, George. "The Theory of Economic Integration and the Experience of the Balkan and Danubian Countries Before 1914." *The Florida State University Slavic Papers*, vol. 1 (1967).

Macesich, George. *World Banking and Finance: Cooperation Versus Conflict*. New York: Praeger, 1984.

Macesich, George. *Yugoslavia: Theory and Practice of Development Planning*. Charlottesville: University Press of Virginia, 1964.

Macesich, George, and F. A. Close. "Comparative Stability of Monetary Velocity and the Investment Multiplier for Austria and Yugoslavia." *F.S.U. Slavic Papers*, vol. 3 (1969).

Macesich, George, ed. with assistance of Rikard Lang and Dragomir Vojnić. *Essays on the Yugoslav Economic Model*. New York: Praeger, 1989.

Malthus, Thomas R. *Essay on the Principle of Population as It Affects the Future Improvement of Society*. Reprint. London: J. M. Dent and Sons, 1951.

Malthus, Thomas R. *Essay on the Principle of Population as It Affects the Future Improvement of Society*. Reprinted with an introduction by M. B. Blaug. Homewood, Ill.: Richard D. Irwin, 1963.

Marc, James G., and Herbert A. Simon. *Organizations*. New York: Wiley, 1958.

Marković, Ljubisav. *Ekonomski Sistem Jugoslavije*. Belgrade: Kosmos, 1977.

Marshall, Alfred. *Principles of Economics*. London: Macmillan, 1930.

Marx, Karl. *Das Kapital*. New York: Modern Library, 1906.

McClanghry, John. "A Visionary of Disunion." *New York Times* 28 December 1991.

McCloskey, Donald N., and J. Richard Zecher. "How the International Gold Standard Worked 1880-1913," in *The Monetary Approach to the Balance of Payments*, edited by Jacob A. Frenkel and Harry G. Johnson, 357-85. Toronto: University of Toronto Press, 1976.

McKinnon, Ronald I. "Optimum Currency Areas." *American Economic Review* (September 1963): 717-25.

Meade, James E. *Problem of Economic Union*. Chicago: University of Chicago Press, 1953.

Meiselman, David, ed. *Varieties of Monetary Experience*. Chicago: University of Chicago Press, 1970.

Menger, Carl. *Problems of Economics and Sociology*. Urbana: University of Illinois, 1963.

Moggridge, Donald, ed. *Collected Writings of John Maynard Keynes, Activities 1940-43.* vol. 23, *External War Finance.* New York and London: Cambridge University Press, 1979.

Mundell, Robert A. "A Theory of Optimum Currency Areas." *American Economic Review* (September 1961): 657-64.

Nelson, Charles R. "Adjustment Lags versus Information Lags: A Test of Alternative Explanations of the Phillips Curve Phenomenon." *Journal of Money, Credit, and Banking* (February 1981): 1-11.

Nurkse, Ragnar. *International Currency Experience.* Geneva: League of Nations, 1944.

Ohlin, Bertil. *International and Interregional Trade.* Cambridge, MA: Harvard University Press, 1935.

Olson, Mancur. *The Rise and Decline of Nations.* New Haven, Conn.: Yale University, 1982.

Pašić, Najdan. *The Socio-Political System of Yugoslavia.* Belgrade: Savez Udruženja Pravnika, 1975.

Pigou, Arthur C. *Aspects of British Economic History, 1918-1925.* New York: Macmillan, 1947.

Pontecorvo, G., R. P. Shay, and A. G. Hart. *Issues in Banking and Monetary Analysis.* New York: Holt, Rinehart, and Winston, 1967.

Pope John Paul II. *Laborem Exercens. [On Human Work].* Paulist Press, 1981.

Pope Leo XIII. *Rerum Novarum. [On Conditions of Labor].* Paulist Press, 1891.

Pope Pius XI, *Quadragesimo Anno.* Paulist Press, 1931.

Powell, Ellis T. *The Evolution of the Money Market, 1385-1915.* London: Frank Cass, 1966.

Pryor, Frederic. *Property and Industrial Organization in Communist and Capitalist Nations.* Bloomington: Indiana University Press, 1973.

Rapoport, Anton, and A. M. Chammah. *Prisoner's Dilemma.* Ann Arbor: University of Michigan Press, 1965.

Ratković, Radoslav. *Osnovi Nauke O Politici.* Belgrade: Institut za Politička Studije, 1977.

Ricardo, David. *The High Rise of Bullion: A Proof of the Depreciation of Bank Notes.* Reprinted in *Works and Correspondence of David Ricardo,* ed. P. Sraffa, Vol. III (Cambridge: Cambridge University Press, 1951; New York: Cambridge University Press, 1973).

Rogin, L. *The Meaning and Validity of Economic Theory.* New York: Harper and Row, 1938.

Roskill, Stephen. *Hankey: Man of Secrets, Volume II: 1919-1931.* Annapolis, Md.: U.S. Naval Institute Press, 1972.

Rourke, Francis E. *Bureaucracy, Politics, and Public Policy.* 2d ed.

Boston: Little, Brown, 1976.

Samuels, Warren J. "Adam Smith and the Economy as a System of Power." *Review of Social Economy* (October 1973): 123-37.

Samuelson, Paul. "Sympathy from the Other Cambridge." *The Economist* 25 June 1983, pp. 19-21.

Say, Jean Baptiste. *Treatise on Political Economy.* Philadelphia: Lippincott, 1863. This translation is from the fourth French edition, published in 1821.

Schmidt, Wilson E. "Commentary" quoted in I. O. Scott's paper in *Issues in Banking and Monetary Analysis,* edited by G. Pontecorvo, R. P. Shay, and A. G. Hart, 203-5. New York: Holt, Rinehart, and Winston, 1967.

Schotter, Andrew. *The Economic Theory of Social Institutions.* Cambridge: Cambridge University Press, 1981.

Schotter, Andrew, and Gerhard Schwodiauer. "Economics and the Theory of Games: A Survey." *Journal of Economic Literature* (June 1980): 479-527.

Schuker, Stephen A. "Review of E. Johnson's *Collected Writings of John Maynard Keynes.*" *Journal of Economic Literature* (March 1980): 124-26.

Schumpeter, J. A. *History of Economic Analysis.* New York: Oxford University Press, 1954.

Schwartz, Anna J. *A Century of British Market Interest Rates 1874-1975.* London: The City University, 1981.

Schwartz, Anna J. "A Review of Explanations of 1929-1933." *Proceedings & Reports of the Center for Yugoslav-American Studies, Research, and Exchanges, Florida State University,* vols. 12-13, edited by George Macesich. Tallahassee: Center for Yugoslav-American Studies, Research, and Exchanges, Florida State University, 1978-1979.

Scitovsky, Tibor. *Economic Theory and Western European Integration.* Stanford, Calif.: Stanford University Press, 1958.

Šefer, Berislav. *Socialni Razvoj u Samoupravnom Društvu.* Belgrade: Institut za Političke Studije FPN, 1971.

Seidman, Harold. *Politics, Position, and Power: The Dynamics of Federal Organization.* 3d ed. New York: Oxford University Press, 1980.

Shaw, G. B., ed. *Fabian Essays.* London: George Allen and Unwin, 1948.

Simon, Herbert A. *Administrative Behavior.* 3d ed. New York: Free Press, 1976.

Smith, Adam. *An Inquiry into the Nature and Causes of the Wealth of Nations.* Reprinted in two volumes, edited by R. H. Campbell, A. S. Skinner, and W. B. Todd. Oxford: Clarendon Press, 1976.

Smith, Lawrence. "England's Return to the Gold Standard in 1925." *Journal of Economic and Business History* (February 1932): 228-58).

Solo, Robert A. "The Neo-Marxist Theory of the State." *Journal of Economic Issues* vol.12, no. 4 (December 1978): 829-42.

Solo, Robert A. *The Positive State.* Cincinnati: South-Western Publishing Co., 1982.

Spencer, H. "Inflation, Unemployment, and Hayek." *Federal Reserve Board of St. Louis Bulletin* (May 1975).

Spengler, J. J. *Origins of Economic Thought and Justice.* Carbondale and Edwardsville: Southern Illinois University, 1980.

Spengler, J. J., and W. R. Allen. *Essays in Economic Thought.* Chicago: Rand McNally, 1960.

Stein, Herbert. *The Fiscal Revolution in America.* Chicago: University of Chicago Press, 1969.

Stigler, George. *Production and Distribution Theories.* New York: Macmillan, 1941.

Streeten, Paul. *Economic Integration: Aspects and Problems.* Leyden: A. W. Sythoff, 1961.

Svennilson, Ingvar. *Growth and Stagnation in the European Economy.* Geneva: United Nations Economic Commission for Europe, 1954.

Sweezy, Paul M. *Socialism.* New York: McGraw-Hill, 1949.

Tabalas, George. "Some Initial Formulations of the Monetary Growth-Rate Rule." *History of Political Economy* (Winter 1977): 525-47.

Tawney, Richard. *Acquisitive Society.* New York: Harcourt, Brace and Dodd, 1960.

Tawney, Richard. *Equality.* New York: Capricorn Books, 1961.

Tawney, Richard. *Religion and the Rise of Capitalism.* New York: Harcourt, Brace, 1926.

Taylor, M. *Anarchy and Cooperation.* New York: John Wiley and Sons, 1976.

Thornton, A. P. *The Imperial Idea and Its Enemies: A Study in British Power.* New York: Auden Books, 1968.

Thornton, Henry. *Enquiry into the Nature and Effects of the Paper Credit of Great Britain.* Edited with an introduction by F. A. Hayek. London: George Allen and Unwin, 1939. Reprint. New York: Augustus Kelley, 1962.

Triffin, Robert. *The Evaluation of the International Monetary System: Historical Reappraisal and Historical Perspectives.* Princeton, N.J.: Princeton University Press, 1965.

Vanek, Jaroslav. *The Participatory Economy: An Evolutionary Hypothesis and a Strategy for Development.* Ithaca, N.Y.: Cornell University Press, 1971.

Veblen, Thorstein. *The Theory of Business Enterprise.* New York:

Augustus M. Kelley, 1965.

Veblen, Thorstein. *The Theory of the Leisure Class*. New York: Modern Library, 1934.

Vickers, D. *Studies in the Theory of Money*. Philadelphia, Chilton Co., 1959.

Viner, J. *Studies in the Theory of International Trade*. New York: Harper and Bros., 1937.

Viner, Jacob. *The Customs Unions Issue*. New York: Carnegie Endowment for International Peace, 1950.

Vinski, Ivo. "Dugoročna kretanja stanovništva i društvenog proizvoda Jugoslavije." In *Aktuelni problemi privredni kretanja i ekonomske politike Jugoslavije*, edited by Dragomir Vojnić, 111-17. Zagreb: Ekonomski Institut and Informator, 1974.

Vinski, Ivo. "Zapošljavanje u inozemstvu i privredni rast Jugoslavije do 1985." In *Aktuelni problemi privredni kretanja i ekonomske politike Jugoslavije*, edited by Dragomir Vojnić, 201-12. Zagreb: Ekonomski Institut and Informator, 1974.

von Mises, Ludwig. *The Anti-Capitalistic Mentality*. New York: Van Nostrand, 1956.

von Mises, Ludwig. *Socialism: An Economic and Sociological Analysis*, translated from German by Jacques Kahane. London: Jonathan Cape, 1936.

Vuchinich, W. S. "Interwar Yugoslavia." In *Contemporary Yugoslavia*, edited by W. S. Vuchinich. Berkeley: University of California Press, 1969.

Walker, David B. *Toward a Functioning Federalism*. Cambridge, Mass.: Winthrop, 1981.

Ward, Benjamin. "The Firm in Illyria: Market Synicalism." *American Economic Review* vol. 48, no. 4 (September 1958).

Warwick, Donald P. *A Theory of Public Bureaucracy*. Cambridge, Mass.: Harvard University Press, 1975.

Waterston, Albert. *Planning in Yugoslavia*. (in mimeographed form).

Weber, Max. *On Charisma and Institution Building–Selected Papers*. Edited with an introduction by S. M. Eisenstadt. Chicago: University of Chicago Press, 1968.

Whitaker, E. *Schools and Streams of Economic Thought*. Chicago: Rand McNally, 1961.

Wildavsky, Aaron. *The Politics of the Budgetary Process*. 2d ed. Boston: Little, Brown, 1974.

Wiles, P.J.D. *Economic Institutions Compared*. New York: Halsted Press, 1977.

Wiles, P.J.D. *The Political Economy of Communism*. Cambridge, Mass.: Harvard University Press, 1962.

Williams, David. "London and the 1931 Financial Crisis." *Economic*

History Review (April 1963): 512-28.

Wilson, James Q. "The Rise of the Bureaucratic State." *The Public Interest* 41 (Fall 1975): 77-103.

Wisely, William. *A Tool of Power: The Political History of Money.* New York: John Wiley and Sons, 1977.

Yeager, Leland B. "Exchange Rates Within a Common Market." *Social Research* (January 1959): 415-38.

Yeager, Leland B. *International Monetary Relations: Theory, History, and Policy, Part II.* New York: Harper and Row, 1966.

Young, Allyn A. "Economics and War." *American Economic Review* (March 1926): 1-13.

Zimbalist, Andrew, and Howard Fuerman. *Comparing Economic Systems: A Political Economic Approach.* New York: Academic Press, 1984.

Index

Anti-Combination Laws, 69
Antitrust policy, 48
Aquinas, Thomas, 80
Austria: Great Depression in, 14; inflation during 1920s in, 5
Austro-Hungarian Empire: attempt to stabilize successor states of, 25–26; break up of, 4
Axelrod, Robert, 35, 37, 38

Bagehot, Walter, 23, 67, 77–78
Banking school, 78–79
Belgium, 14, 15
Bentham, Jeremy, 69, 73–74
Besant, Annie, 81
Bićanić, Rudolf, 127
Bolshevik Revolution, 85
Buchanan, James M., 46
Bukharin, Nikolai, 85
Bureaucracy: accountability and, 102–3; centrally planned economy and, 106; demand for constraints on, 94–95; demand for national-ism by, 98; economic model for behavior of, 100–101; in former socialist countries, 95–96; increas-ing power of, 99–100; as national-ist state, 97–98; political behavior and, 101–2; traditional concepts

of, 102

Canada: economic situation during 1930s in, 19–20; Great Depres-sion in, 8; unemployment in, 57
Cantillon, Richard, 66
Capitalism: description of, 53–54; Marx on, 68, 74–75; Marxist pre-dictions for Western, 97
Catchings, W., 87
Centrally planned economy (CPE): characteristics of, 105–7, 132; explanation of, 105; "not nice" strategy and, 107–9; reform of, 109–10
Churchill, Sir Winston, 17
Classical economics, 68–75
Coase, Ronald H., 46
Commons, John R., 83
Communitarianism: in European countries, 50, 51; explanation of, 49; U.S. political system and, 50
Consumption, adjustment of pro-duction to, 44
Cooperation: arbitrary exercise of authority and, 56; based on reci-procity, 37, 39, 40; evolution of, 35–36; insight offered by theory of, 40; questions regarding, 33;

About the Author

GEORGE MACESICH is Professor of Economics and founding direc-
tor of the Center for Yugoslav-American Studies, Research, and
Exchanges at Florida State University, Tallahassee. He is also author
of over thirty books, including *Monetary Policy and Politics* (Praeger,
1992); *Yugoslavia in the Age of Democracy* (Praeger, 1992); *World Debt
and Stability* (Praeger, 1991); *Money Supply Process*, with D. Dimitrijević (Praeger, 1991); *Monetary Policy and Rational Expectations*
(Praeger, 1987).

ISBN 0-275-94936-2

90000>

9 780275 949365

HARDCOVER BAR CODE